Police Leadership Redefined

Copyright © Gene Reid 2023
All rights reserved.

No part of this book may be reproduced, or stored in a retrieval system, or transmitted in any form or by any means, electronic, mechanical, photocopying, recording, or otherwise, without express written permission of the publisher.

Published by Reid Solutions, LLC.

Cover and interior design by Ian Koviak

ISBN (print) 979-8-8703417-8-1

First printing 2024
Printed in the United States of America

TRANSFORMING LAW ENFORCEMENT
with EMOTIONAL INTELLIGENCE

Police Leadership

Redefined

THE EQ ADVANTAGE

Gene Reid, Ph.D.

Public Praise

Police Leadership Redefined: The EQ Advantage is a compelling and thought-provoking resource about fostering a deeper understanding of ourselves as a significant investment in our own growth as law enforcement leaders. This book illustrates the signature qualities of success for true servant leaders.

Chief Patrick Ogden
ASSOCIATE VICE PRESIDENT, UNIVERSITY OF DELAWARE POLICE

Every person should read this book- not just leaders, not just police officers, and not just men. It's not just theory, but practical tips on how we can all be more aware of ourselves and the roles we play on teams or in our families.

Betsy Renzo, Esq.
EXECUTIVE DIRECTOR, DELAWARE LAW RELATED EDUCATION CENTER

This book should be a mandatory read for all law enforcement supervisors. Dr. Reid masterfully explains the importance of blending self-awareness, self-management, social awareness, and relationship management into modern day police supervision.

Brian Grant
SPECIAL AGENT

Police Leadership Redefined: The EQ Advantage is an insightful read that offers a fresh perspective on law enforcement leadership through the lens of emotional intelligence. This book is a must-read for law enforcement professionals seeking to enhance their leadership skills and foster a positive work environment.

Nancy Perry
EDITOR-IN-CHIEF, POLICE1

To Abby, Laila, and Luke,
For your love, inspiration, and unwavering support.
With all my love,
—*Gene*

Disclaimer

This book unearths the synergy of emotions and leadership. If you believe they don't naturally align, this book is tailored for you. Open your mind to the exploration of how emotions can profoundly impact and enhance leadership effectiveness.

Order *of* Operations

Introduction 13
The Why 20
Background 22

SECTION I. SELF-AWARENESS 29
Duty and Discord 31
Emotional Sudoku 36
Primary Targets 39
   Keep a Journal 40
   Pay Attention 42
   Be Curious 46
   Gather Insights 49
Calm Amidst the Chaos 54
Debrief 57

SECTION II. SELF-MANAGEMENT 59
Brewing Discontent 63
Embrace the Wave 65
Primary Targets 66
   Breathe 68
   Get Moving 71
   Spring Cleaning 73
   Discipline 75
Mayhem Mastery 82
Debrief 83

SECTION III. SOCIAL AWARENESS ... 83
An Unspoken Battle ... 85
Room Reconnaissance ... 89
Primary Targets ... 91
    Just Listen ... 92
    Step Back and Watch ... 94
    Be Social ... 96
    Exchange Perspectives ... 98
Unity in Turbulence ... 101
Debrief ... 105

SECTION IV. RELATIONSHIP MANAGEMENT ... 107
Sergeant's Slide ... 109
Navigating Bonds ... 117
Primary Targets ... 121
    Fix It ... 122
    First Name Basis ... 125
    Speak Up ... 127
    Be Authentic ... 129
Dual Duties ... 131
Debrief ... 137

Moving Forward ... 139
Reading Suggestions ... 140
About the Author ... 141

Introduction

ON THE RIGHT SIDE
A Path *to* Leadership

Captain Luke Anderson steered his unmarked SUV through the early morning traffic, the subtle hum of the engine blending with the city's awakening sounds. A middle-aged figure, he sported a military-style haircut that seemed to defy the chaos of the morning rush. Every strand in place, his appearance hinted at a disciplined precision that extended beyond his grooming.

The rising sun cast a warm embrace over the city, illuminating the contours of his face marked by experience. Despite his slim build, there was an undeniable sense of authority in the way he gripped the steering wheel, navigating the familiar streets with a practiced ease. As he pondered the day ahead, his mind danced between anticipation and reflection, and the city bore witness to the arrival of a man whose physical presence embodied a quiet but formidable strength.

His thoughts turned to the upcoming roll call, where he was scheduled to address the officers under his command that morning. Luke had always taken these moments seriously. It was a chance to inspire and motivate the officers, setting the tone for the weeks ahead. The impending discussion carried a heavier burden than usual for Luke. He aimed to draw from his own law enforcement background, offering personal insights to counter the undercurrents of low morale spurred by staffing shortages and a surge in crime—issues that city officials were demanding solutions for.

Amid a whirlwind of thoughts, Luke's mind settled on the cherished scenes of the breakfast table back home. A vivid image unfolded before him – Ryan, his vibrant red hair reflecting the morning light, and Emily, with her golden blonde locks, seated at the kitchen counter just minutes ago. The warm glow of the morning sun painted their faces with a soft radiance.

The delightful aroma of pancakes and fresh coffee lingered in his memories, evoking a profound sense of longing. These were the moments that Luke held dear, snapshots of the simple joys shared with his two children. Ryan, a spirited 4-year-old with a mop of red hair, brought an infectious energy to the morning ritual. His laughter echoed through the house, turning ordinary moments into lively adventures.

Six-year-old Emily, with her nurturing spirit and blonde hair that matched the morning sunlight, took on the role of a caring older sister. Her imaginative soul turned the breakfast table into a stage for playful arguments and shared giggles. Mornings, for Luke, were a time to witness the unique bond between his kids as they playfully bickered over the last pancake or shared a cereal-induced laugh.

Luke cherished those precious moments with his family, the simple joys of watching his kids giggle over their cereal or argue playfully about who got the last pancake. A frown creased his forehead as he recalled the necessity of leaving early. A routine that often left him feeling torn. The tug-of-war between professional duty and personal desire was a familiar struggle. Luke hated the idea of missing those breakfasts, the chance to share a few more laughs and words of encouragement before the day pulled him away.

The radio crackled to life, interrupting his thoughts as he pulled into the parking lot. Stepping out of his SUV, Luke took a deep breath, the crisp morning air invigorating him. With a determined stride, he made his way through the bustling police department, acknowledging officers by their first names as he passed. A warm smile adorned his face, an effort to infuse a positive energy into the atmosphere.

"Good morning, Mike," he greeted a seasoned officer at the entrance, clapping him on the shoulder. "Ready for another day of keeping the city safe?"

Mike grinned in response, nodding appreciatively. "Always, Captain."

Luke chuckled, a lighthearted tone in his voice. "Well, someone's got to. Let's make it count today."

As he walked through the halls, he continued to exchange pleasantries with officers, stopping to chat briefly about family, hobbies, or the latest developments in their lives. Luke knew the importance of fostering a sense of camaraderie within the department. It wasn't just about enforcing the law. It was about building a community within the organization.

He reached his office, a space adorned with commendations, family photos, and a map of the city. Luke's gaze hovered on the pictures of his wife and kids, a momentary pause in his brisk walk. With a sigh, he collected himself and opened the door.

"Morning, Captain!" his secretary, Lisa Goldstein, greeted him with a bright smile.

"Good morning, Lisa!" Luke returned the smile, appreciating her efficiency and positive demeanor. "Any messages for me?"

"Just the usual," she replied, handing him a stack of papers. "And don't forget, Chief Stevens wants to see you after roll call."

Luke nodded, making a mental note. "Thanks, Lisa. By the way, how's that cat of yours doing?"

A surprised look crossed Lisa's face, followed by a laugh. "Captain, you know Mittens. She's causing trouble as usual."

"Well, give her my regards," Luke said, chuckling as he stepped into his office.

The roll call loomed ahead, but Luke felt a renewed sense of purpose. The interactions in the hallway had set a positive tone, and he was ready to share his experiences with the officers. With a final glance at the photos on his desk, he squared his shoulders, ready to inspire and motivate his team for the challenges that lie ahead.

The department's roll call meeting was somber, the burden of recent challenges palpable in the air. Luke stood at the front of the room, his expression conveying a resolute demeanor.

Positioned at the front, Lieutenant Megan Turner, looking somewhat disheveled, barely acknowledged his presence as he entered the room.

"Rough morning, Lieutenant?" Luke asked, attempting to read her mood with a touch of humor.

Megan responded with a subtle but clear display of exasperation, "You could say that. Some of us aren't morning people."

Luke chuckled. "Noted. Let's turn this ship around, shall we?" He addressed the room, injecting a bit of levity.

"Good morning, everyone," Luke began, his tone measured

but empathetic. "I've heard some rumblings about a dip in morale lately, and I want to address it head-on. Policing is tough, and we're facing some serious challenges. Staffing sure isn't helping. But it's crucial that we support each other through thick and thin." He scanned the room, making eye contact with each officer. "I know the workload has been heavy, I'm meeting with Chief Stevens today to get you some more support out there. Your dedication does not go unnoticed. Each one of you plays a vital role in keeping this city safe."

Upon hearing Luke's words, an audible scoff emanated from the back of the room. A portly man, sporting a borderline 5 o'clock shadow, kept a fixed gaze on the clock, clearly irritated by the captain's presence. Corporal Frank Martin, a seasoned and skeptical veteran of the force who had witnessed his fair share of speeches in the roll call room, projected his doubt. Luke, understanding the skepticism, made deliberate eye contact with him as he spoke, aiming to quell the behavior. The attention of the officers was shifting towards Corporal Martin, and Luke wanted to ensure they focused on his message instead. He would have to address Corporal Martin personally in the very near future.

As he continued, Luke began acknowledging individual officers by name, recounting specific instances where their efforts had made a difference, and reminisced about his time spent on the road as a patrol officer. He spoke of their commitment, bravery, and resilience, highlighting the positive impact they had on the community.

"And let me be clear," Luke emphasized, "your well-being matters. If anyone is feeling overwhelmed, don't hesitate to reach out. We're a team, and we look out for each other."

As the roll call meeting concluded, the atmosphere in the room had shifted. Officers exchanged nods and supportive glances, realizing they were not alone in facing the challenges of their profession. Luke's acknowledgment of their efforts and his commitment to addressing the morale issue had planted the seeds for a more supportive and cohesive team.

After the roll call meeting, Luke noticed Officer Jake Thompson, a young officer with a determined yet slightly weary expression. As officers filed out of the room, Luke caught up with Jake in the hallway.

"Hey, Jake, mind walking with me to the parking lot for a moment?" Luke asked, a friendly tone in his voice.

Surprised but eager, Jake nodded and fell into step beside the captain. They walked in companionable silence for a few moments before Luke spoke.

"I've been impressed with your dedication and work ethic, Jake. You're handling some tough cases, and I can see the effort you're putting in," the captain said, genuine appreciation in his eyes.

Jake, taken aback by the captain's personalized attention, managed a grateful smile. "Thank you, sir. It means a lot."

"I know it's not easy, especially for someone newer to the road. But I wanted you to know that you're doing the job better than I did at your age. You're making a difference here, and I believe in your potential," Luke continued, patting Jake on the shoulder.

Jake felt a wave of revitalized determination, pushing aside his fatigue. "I appreciate that, Captain. It's been tough out there," he admitted, his gaze shifting across the parking lot to a group of officers as they filed out of the building.

"I get it, Jake. We're a team, and we need each other. If there's ever anything you need or if you just want to talk, my door is always open. Your well-being matters as much as your performance out there," Luke reassured him.

As they arrived at Jake's car, Luke extended a handshake. "Keep up the good stuff, Officer Thompson. It won't be long before you're gunning for my position," he quipped, a lighthearted tone accompanying his words.

Jake, now more than just another officer in the ranks, felt a surge of motivation. Luke's words had not only acknowledged his efforts but had made him feel like a valued member of the team. It was a small gesture, but it left a lasting impact on Jake's morale and sense of belonging within the department.

WHAT IS IT?

While Captain Luke Anderson may have studied countless leadership theories, reviewed relevant books on the subject, and participated in the top leadership courses, it's unlikely that he possesses superhuman leadership abilities. The question arises: What specific skill set has Luke cultivated to exert such a discernible influence on the officers in that roll call room?

Luckily, it's much simpler than you might imagine. Captain Luke Anderson possesses a significant level of *emotional intelligence*. While mastering this essential skillset isn't a straightforward task, it is achievable with dedication, education, and time.

The Why

True leadership transcends titles. The essence of your leadership is measured by the inspiration you ignite in others, not by the title you hold. The ultimate goal is not to command, but to empower others to discover the leaders within themselves. I strongly believe that occupying a leadership position, be it formal or informal, comes with an unequivocal obligation to pursue greatness relentlessly— there is simply no alternative.

Imperfections are woven into my own leadership journey, and I make no claims of perfection. Nevertheless, my unwavering dedication persists in the unyielding pursuit of self-improvement, a passage where the goal is constant refinement and growth. In my academic and professional career, I have consistently observed that elevated emotional intelligence is a key indicator of true leadership. Consequently, making a concerted effort to elevate my own emotional intelligence has been a meaningful pursuit. This is underscored by my development of this content, crafted to assist leaders in improving their skills.

As we embark on exploring emotional intelligence together, the cornerstone of great leadership, it will become evident that understanding its significance is only a preliminary step. The transformative impact occurs when you make the decision to actively integrate emotional intelligence into your leadership style, translating knowledge into tangible actions that foster positive relationships and outcomes.

The insights I offer are drawn from practical experiences, including both my own triumphs and failures, as well as observations of others. Within the tales awaiting you, fiction takes center stage, yet amid every crafted narrative lies a subtle glint of truth, ensuring a unique blend of imagination and reality. As we explore targeted goals to improve various aspects of emotional intelligence, know that I have personally implemented these strategies, and they have proven to be effective.

My goal isn't to reinvent the wheel and overhaul the well-established body of literature on emotional intelligence. Numerous resources are available for exploration, and you're encouraged to delve into the works of industry pioneers. Examples include Daniel Goleman's book *Emotional Intelligence: Why It Can Matter More Than IQ*, as well as the contributions of Travis Bradberry and Jean Greaves, encompassing titles like *The Emotional Intelligence Quick Book* and *Emotional Intelligence 2.0*.

Rather than dissecting every detail or exploring all the possibilities within the vast realm of emotional intelligence, my goal is to provide a guide specifically crafted for police leaders looking to enhance their emotional intelligence. To streamline the process, I've compiled some artfully crafted stories to vividly illustrate the complexities of emotional intelligence. This guide will also offer valuable insights to aid in the improvement of your own proficiency.

Background

Before we dive into the exciting bits, let's take a detour into the roots of emotional intelligence. Consider it the backstage pass to give your understanding a rock-solid foundation.

Emotional intelligence (EQ) is a complex and multi-dimensional concept that encompasses the ability to recognize, understand, manage, and utilize one's own emotions effectively, while also being attuned to the emotions of others. It extends beyond traditional measures of intelligence and plays a crucial role in interpersonal relationships, communication, and overall well-being.

It's vital for you to grasp early on that emotional intelligence comprises four key elements: self-awareness, self-management, social awareness, and relationship management. These areas are interconnected, meaning strong relationship management skills hinge on possessing self-awareness, self-management abilities, and social awareness. Equally significant is the understanding that a lack of self-awareness, our first area of focus after exploring the origins of EQ, will hinder progress in the remaining three areas.

YOU MIGHT HAVE COME ACROSS THE ACRONYMS EI AND EQ IN DISCUSSIONS ON EMOTIONAL INTELLIGENCE. WHILE BOTH ABBREVIATIONS ARE VALID, I PERSONALLY FAVOR EQ. EMOTIONAL INTELLIGENCE AND INTELLIGENCE QUOTIENT (IQ) ARE FREQUENTLY DISCUSSED TOGETHER, INFLUENCING MY PREFERENCE FOR EQ AS A REPRESENTATION OF EMOTIONAL INTELLIGENCE. BOTH CHOICES ARE CORRECT, SO FEEL FREE TO USE THE ONE THAT ALIGNS WITH YOUR PREFERENCE IN FUTURE DISCUSSIONS.

Origins of Emotional Intelligence

The origins of emotional intelligence can be traced back to the early 20th century, but it garnered widespread attention in the 1990s with the introduction of the term by psychologists Peter Salovey and John Mayer. However, it was the work of Daniel Goleman, through his book *Emotional Intelligence: Why It Can Matter More Than IQ*, published in 1995, that brought widespread attention to the idea.

Salovey and Mayer initially defined emotional intelligence as the ability to perceive, understand, manage, and regulate emotions – both one's own and those of others. They proposed a model consisting of four branches: perception of emotion, using emotion to facilitate thought, understanding emotion, and managing emotion.

Goleman took these concepts to the next level, bringing them into the spotlight by highlighting the real-world applications of emotional intelligence across different life domains. Additionally, credit goes to Goleman for dissecting emotional intelligence into four key categories: self-awareness, self-management, social awareness, and relationship management.

Travis Bradberry and Jean Greaves have left a significant mark in the arena of emotional intelligence with their impactful works, including the *Emotional Intelligence Quick Book* and *Emotional Intelligence 2.0*. Their unique perspective has injected fresh insights into the subject, resonating with readers and enriching the ongoing conversation about the vital role of emotional intelligence in both personal and professional growth.

IQ v EQ

We're on the brink of escaping the mundane, but don't bail just yet. Spoiler alert: IQ isn't the MVP your teachers raved about. The real headliner is about to steal the spotlight.

In tracing the origins of emotional intelligence, it's essential to recognize the influence of Howard Gardner's theory of multiple intelligences. Gardner proposed that intelligence is not a singular entity measured solely through IQ tests but comprises various forms, including interpersonal and intrapersonal intelligence. This notion laid the groundwork for the broader acceptance of emotional intelligence as a valuable aspect of human cognition and behavior.

Intelligence Quotient (IQ) and Emotional Intelligence (EQ) represent distinct facets of cognitive and social capabilities, and their impact on leadership effectiveness varies significantly. While IQ measures intellectual abilities and cognitive skills, EQ focuses on the realm of emotions, interpersonal relationships, and self-awareness. In the context of leadership, the discussion often leans towards EQ as a more critical factor for success.

REMEMBER CAPTAIN LUKE ANDERSON? HIS ABILITY TO SMOOTHLY ADDRESS MORALE ISSUES DURING ROLL CALL AND SEAMLESSLY TRANSITION TO MAKING A YOUNG OFFICER FEEL GENUINELY VALUED AND APPRECIATED WAS REMARKABLE. WHILE HE UNDENIABLY POSSESSES A COMMENDABLE LEVEL OF IQ, IT WAS HIS EXCEPTIONAL CAPACITY TO ACKNOWLEDGE THE SIGNIFICANCE OF ESTABLISHING CONNECTIONS WITH OFFICERS IN THE ROLL CALL ROOM AND EFFECTIVELY EXECUTING THIS ABILITY THAT RENDERED HIS ACTIONS PROFOUNDLY IMPACTFUL.

Leadership is inherently a social endeavor, requiring the ability to connect with and influence others. IQ, while valuable for problem-solving and analytical thinking, may not fully equip leaders with the interpersonal skills necessary to navigate complex human dynamics. In contrast, EQ encompasses self-awareness, self-regulation, social awareness, and relationship management—traits that are pivotal for effective leadership.

Leaders with high EQ possess a keen understanding of their own emotions, allowing them to remain composed in high-pressure situations. This self-awareness extends to an understanding of how emotions influence decision-making, enabling leaders to make choices that resonate with their team. Also, social awareness, a key component of EQ, fosters better communication and collaboration, contributing to a positive and cohesive organizational culture.

In dynamic and diverse work environments, where collaboration and adaptability are paramount, leaders with elevated EQ are often better equipped to navigate challenges. They excel in conflict resolution, are attuned to the needs of their team members, and can create an inclusive and supportive atmosphere. While a high IQ is undoubtedly beneficial, it is the integration of emotional intelligence that elevates leaders from being technically proficient to truly inspirational and transformative.

While IQ lays the foundation for cognitive prowess, EQ enhances a leader's ability to connect, inspire, and lead effectively. In today's leadership landscape, where empathy and adaptability are increasingly valued, emotional intelligence emerges as a critical differentiator, often outweighing the sole reliance on intellectual capacities measured by IQ. The most successful leaders often strike a delicate balance between IQ and EQ, recognizing that both are integral, but it is the latter that often proves indispensable in navigating the intricate terrain of human relationships and leadership challenges.

FOUR PILLARS OF EMOTIONAL INTELLIGENCE

Emotional intelligence is often broken down into four primary components, each playing a distinct role in shaping an individual's emotional acumen:

REMEMBER THAT EACH OF THE FOUR PILLARS ARE INTERCONNECTED, SUPPORTING ONE ANOTHER. ACHIEVING EXCELLENCE IN RELATIONSHIP MANAGEMENT IS CHALLENGING IF YOUR SELF-AWARENESS IS NOT WELL-DEVELOPED.

- **Self-Awareness:**
    This involves recognizing and understanding one's own emotions, including their impact on thoughts, behavior, and decision-making. Self-awareness forms the base layer for developing other emotional intelligence skills.
- **Self-Management:**
    Building on self-awareness, self-management involves the ability to regulate and control one's emotions in various situations. It includes resilience in the face of challenges, adaptability, and the capacity to remain composed under pressure.
- **Social Awareness:**
    Social awareness entails perceiving and understanding the emotions of others. This component involves empathy, the skill to recognize and appreciate different perspectives, and an awareness of the emotional dynamics within a group or social setting.
- **Relationship Management:**
    The final component, relationship management, focuses on leveraging emotional intelligence to navigate and enhance interpersonal connections. This includes effective communication, conflict resolution, and the ability to build and maintain positive relationships.

Together, these components form a holistic framework for emotional intelligence, providing individuals with the tools to navigate the complexities of their own emotions and those of the people around them. Developing proficiency in each component can lead to more fulfilling relationships, improved leadership skills, and overall personal and professional success.

Keep in mind that each of these four areas should progress in sequence. The foundation is laid with self-awareness, which we will investigate next.

SECTION 1

Self-Awareness

Duty *and* Discord

Lieutenant Megan Turner groaned as the blaring sound of her alarm clock shattered the remnants of a restless night's sleep. The digital numbers on the clock mocked her, displaying an ungodly hour that seemed to scream, "It's too early for this." Megan rubbed her tired eyes, trying to shake off the drowsiness that clung to her like a persistent shadow.

Last night had been rough. Her daughter, Maggie, had been up with a bout of restlessness, tossing and turning throughout the night. Megan had spent hours trying to comfort her, soothing her daughter's troubled dreams, and navigating the challenges of parenthood. As she dragged herself out of bed, Megan couldn't help but long for a few more hours of precious sleep.

In the dim light of the bedroom, Megan caught a glimpse of her husband, Adam, carefully dressing their toddler, Maggie, in her daycare clothes. Megan's heart swelled with a mix of love and guilt. She wished she could spend more time with her family, but duty called, and the city needed its protectors.

Adam, sensing Megan's tiredness, offered a sympathetic smile. "I've got Maggie today. You focus on catching the bad guys, Lieutenant," he said, giving Megan an encouraging smile as he gently touched her forehead.

Megan mustered a tired smile in return, silently grateful for a supportive partner who understood the demands of her job. As she watched Adam and Maggie leave, her hand subconsciously reached for the hair clip on the dresser. A delicate accessory, it had been a gift from Adam during happier, less stressful times.

In the midst of gathering her hair into a tight bun, the clip betrayed her, snapping with an audible crack. Megan sighed, frustration etching lines on her face. She surveyed herself in the mirror, contemplating whether to redo her hair or embrace the slightly disheveled look.

Time was of the essence, and duty awaited. Megan took a deep breath, deciding to leave her hair as it was. The broken clip served as a tangible reminder of the wear and tear that came with her role as a police lieutenant. As she fastened her badge onto her crisp uniform, Megan steeled herself for the challenges that lay ahead.

Megan walked into the crowded roll call room, her usually composed demeanor marred by the visible strain plastered across her face. The department had been grappling with staffing issues and unsolved crime sprees, and Megan was feeling the pressure. Unknown to everyone else in the room, personal challenges at home, including sleepless nights with a restless child, had exacerbated the lieutenant's stress.

As the roll call proceeded, Megan's frustration with the persistent staffing issues, and perceived pressure from the community to increase patrols in the high crime areas, reached a tipping point. The room felt the brunt of her irritation as she sharply addressed the officers, "We're stretched thin, and I can't keep covering for everyone. Don't expect to have any more vacation slots approved. We need all the bodies we can get."

Sergeant Eric Johnson exchanged a concerned glance with

Corporal Lance Edwards, both sensing an unusual intensity in the lieutenant's tone. During a break, Sergeant Johnson approached Megan privately, expressing his concern. "Lieutenant, feel free to tell me to buzz off, but I've kind of noticed some tension today. Obviously, something is going on."

Megan, however, dismissed the concerns from the dedicated sergeant with a wave of her hand. "This is the job. We all signed up for it. If you can't handle the pressure, maybe it's time to find something else. Haven't we all heard that before? I'm fine."

Megan's lack of self-awareness regarding the personal turmoil impacting her emotions became increasingly apparent. Unbeknownst to her, the mounting stress from home, compounded by the lack of sleep, had blurred the lines between professional frustration and personal struggles.

A hush descended upon the room when Corporal Edwards, a seasoned veteran known for his straightforwardness, broke the silence during roll call. "Lieutenant, we all understand the staffing challenges, but the way it's being managed is affecting morale. I'm no counselor," Corporal Edwards added, injecting a touch of humor to diffuse the tension, "but what's gotten into you?"

Megan, however, grew defensive. "This isn't the time or place for personal matters. We have a job to do. Let's focus on that and get through this shift."

A muted and uninspiring atmosphere in the room snuffed out any glimmer of hope.

As soon as she concluded her remarks, Captain Luke Anderson strode into the roll call room. Megan had entirely slipped his presence from her mind. "Of all the days, he chooses today to show up?" she muttered to herself not recalling the email confirmation that had been sent the week prior. Uncertain whether she should call the room to attention, Megan opted for a sheepish nod in Captain Anderson's direction.

Captain Anderson possessed a knack for rallying the troops. However, as he began speaking, Megan found herself absorbed in her phone, her attention only diverted when the captain's booming voice interrupted her thoughts. "Anything you'd like to add, Lieutenant?" he inquired, snapping her back to the present.

Megan trudged through the door of her modest home. Her shoulders slumped with exhaustion. The day's frustrations weighed heavily on her, and the weight seemed to double with each step. She could still hear the echoes of missed communication and failed maneuvers in the roll call room that spilled over into the rest of the shift.

Her husband, Adam, looked up from the couch, sensing the tension in the air. "Long day, huh?" he said, trying to break the ice while holding their daughter, Maggie.

Megan let out a sigh, running a hand through her disheveled hair. "You have no idea," she replied, sinking into the armchair opposite Adam. "I can't figure out why the squad isn't performing. It's like they're not clicking, and I can't put my finger on it."

Adam nodded sympathetically. "Well, you can't control everything, you know? Maybe they just need some time to gel."

"I know, I know," Megan said, frustration evident in her voice. "But we don't have time. The city council won't stop talking about the shooting from last weekend, and I just don't have the bodies to cover every single area that needs attention. I don't know what to do. Maybe I wasn't ready for this."

The conversation shifted when Adam noticed the overflowing trash can in the corner of the room. "Hey, did you forget to take out the trash again?" he asked, a hint of annoyance in his tone.

Megan's tired eyes narrowed, and a spark of frustration ignited. "Seriously? You're bringing up the trash now?"

Adam shrugged his shoulders, equally frustrated. "Well, it's a simple thing. If you can't handle the small stuff at home, how are you supposed to handle a squad at work?"

Megan felt a surge of anger, her exhaustion turning into defensiveness. "You think I don't know how to handle things? This has nothing to do with the trash!"

The argument escalated, each word becoming a weapon in the war of frustration that had taken hold of Megan. The real issue, the magnitude of her responsibilities, the fear of failure—all of it poured out in the guise of a mundane household disagreement.

Emotional Sudoku

I can't deny that I've had my fair share of arguments over what seemed like trivial matters, such as the "trash." In truth, it's always a lack of self-awareness that prevents us from realizing the real issue at hand had nothing to do with the trash.

The cornerstone of emotional intelligence is self-awareness, encompassing your capacity to acknowledge and comprehend your own emotions, thoughts, and behaviors. It goes beyond merely being conscious of your emotional state in the moment. It extends to a deeper understanding of the factors influencing those emotions, including your personal values, strengths, weaknesses, and triggers.

AS WE SAW WITH LIEUTENANT MEGAN TURNER, HER LACK OF SELF-AWARENESS—NECESSARY FOR HER TO RECOGNIZE THAT HER SHORTENED TEMPER AND GENERAL DISPLEASURE WERE SIGNIFICANTLY INFLUENCED BY PERSONAL MATTERS—RESULTED IN A CHAIN REACTION OF NEGATIVE EMOTIONS THROUGHOUT THE ROLL CALL ROOM.

As your self-awareness expands, you gain the skill to tune into your emotional responses, empowering you to navigate situations with heightened control and intentionality. This self-reflection is the starting point for the other facets of emotional intelligence because understanding your emotions forms the groundwork for effective self-management, social awareness, and relationship management.

As a self-aware individual, you can pinpoint how your emotions impact your decisions, communication, and interactions with others. This elevated awareness allows you to adapt your behavior in alignment with your goals and values, fostering a more positive and productive social environment.

It's crucial for us to consider that Lieutenant Turner isn't inherently to blame for feeling fatigued due to insufficient sleep and other personal issues—these challenges are widespread and can affect nearly everyone at some point. However, as a leader, it's critical for you to accurately identify the sources of your emotions and channel your reactions through the lens of self-awareness to maintain order and respect. Having a tough day doesn't justify subjecting others to the consequences. Acknowledging your emotions and understanding their origins marks the first step toward mastering emotional intelligence.

At the core of the emotional intelligence framework, self-awareness stands as the bedrock for cultivating emotional intelligence. It provides the groundwork upon which you can develop and enhance your abilities to navigate the complexities of human emotions, both within yourself and in your interactions with others.

Primary Targets *for* Self-Awareness

Keep *a* Journal

Trust me, I get it. The notion of keeping a journal might raise a few eyebrows. Yet, consider it a strategic move rather than a touchy-feely one. Journaling isn't about pouring your heart out like a teenage poet. It's about enhancing self-awareness and honing that elusive skill called emotional intelligence.

JOURNALING ISN'T ABOUT POURING YOUR HEART OUT LIKE A TEENAGE POET. IT'S ABOUT ENHANCING SELF-AWARENESS AND HONING THAT ELUSIVE SKILL CALLED EMOTIONAL INTELLIGENCE.

Your journal serves as a confidential space for you to dissect the day's encounters, providing a detailed account of your professional journey. It's not about baring your soul. It's about capturing the nuances of your decision-making process, analyzing reactions, and recognizing patterns. What went well during that intense interaction, and what could have been handled more adeptly? Documenting these details offers a valuable mirror to your actions, fostering self-awareness by allowing you to step back and objectively evaluate your performance.

Specifically, focus on noting instances that triggered emotional responses. Did a particular situation evoke frustration, empathy, or perhaps a sense of urgency? Documenting these emotional reactions is the key to mastering your own emotional intelligence. By understanding the root causes of your emotions, you empower yourself to navigate future challenges more skillfully. This isn't about overanalyzing feelings. Instead, you are cultivating an acute awareness of the emotional landscape inherent in law enforcement.

Consider your journal as a repository for insights. Record the details that may escape memory over time – the subtle cues in a suspect's behavior, the stressors that influence your decision-making, or the moments that challenge your resilience. Regularly reviewing these entries allows you to identify trends, strengths, and areas for improvement, offering a roadmap for personal and professional development.

Your journal is a silent partner in your continuous journey toward self-awareness and emotional intelligence. Embrace the practice of documenting not just the events, but the emotions and reflections associated with them. It's an investment in your own growth as a leader in the demanding and ever-evolving field of law enforcement.

Pay Attention

In the world of law enforcement, where chaos is the norm, honing emotional intelligence can feel like trying to find a needle in a haystack. But let's break it down—think of it as becoming your own detective, deciphering the emotional clues within.

Consider mindfulness as your secret weapon. Picture yourself, not in a meditation dojo, but taking a moment to breathe. It's not about becoming a Zen master. It's about tuning into your thoughts and emotions amidst the daily hustle.

Now, active listening is your undercover skill. Imagine being the detective who not only hears the words but decodes the emotions behind them. It's like turning up the volume on the radio, catching the emotional frequencies.

IMAGINE BEING THE DETECTIVE WHO NOT ONLY HEARS THE WORDS BUT DECODES THE EMOTIONS BEHIND THEM. IT'S LIKE TURNING UP THE VOLUME ON THE RADIO, CATCHING THE EMOTIONAL FREQUENCIES.

And then, there's the art of self-reflection. No superhero poses needed, just a moment at your desk with a journal, unraveling the mysteries of your day. It's about understanding your reactions, identifying patterns, and continuously evolving.

Carefully treading down the path of self-awareness, you emerge as the silent champion—no capes required, just a skillful navigator through the intricate emotional landscapes of law enforcement. Here's to you, the emotional intelligence investigator, deciphering emotions one enlightening moment after another.

Be Curious

In the intricate journey of cultivating self-awareness, a simple yet powerful tool often overlooked is the practice of asking yourself "why." This probing question serves as a key to unlocking the layers of your thoughts, emotions, and behaviors, laying the groundwork for heightened self-awareness—an indispensable component of emotional intelligence.

Now, I promise, this isn't an attempt to turn you into a philosopher during your coffee break, but it might just be the key to leveling up your leadership game. I'm also not suggesting you embrace the "eternal toddler" mode, where every answer leads to another "why". We're aiming for a touch more sophistication than a preschool interrogation here.

Frequent introspection, guided by the question "why," enables you to uncover the root causes of your reactions, decisions, and feelings. For example, in a professional setting, when faced with a challenging task, questioning why a particular assignment triggers stress or excitement can unearth deeper insights. Is it the fear of failure, the desire for recognition, or perhaps the alignment with your personal values that fuels these emotions? By questioning the motivations behind your emotional responses, you can decipher the intricate web of your psyche.

For instance, imagine you're in the thick of a challenging operation, stress levels soaring higher than a cat stuck in a tree. Instead of diving headfirst into the chaos, ask yourself, "Why does this task make my heart race faster than a rookie in a high-speed pursuit?" Maybe it's the paperwork avalanche looming on the horizon or the thrill of outsmarting the unexpected. Uncovering the "why" can be your stress-management secret weapon.

Similarly, in interpersonal interactions, asking yourself "why" proves invaluable. When confronted with conflict or disagreement, pausing to question the underlying emotions provides a pathway to understanding. For instance, if a colleague's comment triggers irritation, asking why that specific remark evokes such a reaction may reveal personal sensitivities or unresolved issues. This self-inquiry fosters emotional intelligence by unraveling the complexities of your emotional landscape.

The exploration of "why" can serve as a guide for harmonizing your actions with personal values. When standing at the crossroads of career decisions, that bewildering intersection that even your GPS wants to escape, take a moment to ponder, "What makes this career path so enticing?" Whether it's the call of justice or the allure of fresh challenges, grasping your "why" ensures that you're not merely pursuing illusions but remaining steadfast to your core values. Questioning why a certain path is appealing or unappealing can illuminate whether the decision aligns with your aspirations and values.

This self-awareness forms the bedrock for making informed and emotionally intelligent choices in both professional and personal spheres.

BY BUILDING THIS INTROSPECTIVE MUSCLE, YOU ENHANCE YOUR ABILITY TO RECOGNIZE PATTERNS, MOTIVATIONS, AND TRIGGERS, FOSTERING A DEEPER UNDERSTANDING OF YOURSELF—A CORNERSTONE OF EMOTIONAL INTELLIGENCE.

The habit of asking yourself "why" acts as a continuous feedback loop, facilitating an ongoing dialogue with your own thoughts and emotions. By building this introspective muscle, you enhance your ability to recognize patterns, motivations, and triggers, fostering a deeper understanding of yourself—a cornerstone of emotional intelligence. The intentional pursuit of self-awareness through the simple question "why" sets the stage for more deliberate, adaptive, and emotionally intelligent responses in the complex tapestry of human experiences.

Gather Insights

Seeking feedback is like adding spice to a dish – it might sting a bit, but oh, the flavor it brings to your self-awareness feast!

In leadership positions, the focus typically centers on strength and resilience, casting a shadow of skepticism over the notion of seeking feedback. It's no small feat. It requires a considerable amount of courage. Yet, view this act of seeking feedback as a profound stride toward elevating your self-awareness and honing your emotional intelligence, especially within your leadership responsibilities.

To ask for feedback is to willingly enter a space of vulnerability, recognizing the potential for improvement. It's like navigating through unexplored terrain, where the landscape is unpredictable, and the outcome remains uncertain. In the domain of policing, where decisiveness is highly valued, expressing the desire for emotional and professional growth can be perceived as a departure from the conventional norm.

TO ASK FOR FEEDBACK IS TO WILLINGLY ENTER A SPACE OF VULNERABILITY, RECOGNIZING THE POTENTIAL FOR IMPROVEMENT.

The bravery needed to ask for feedback is comparable to confronting the unknown, much like entering a dim alley during a late-night patrol. It requires putting aside the shield of invulnerability, realizing that you have areas for development. This recognition demands a level of introspection that, at times, can be as challenging as diffusing a tense situation.

While it's understandable to hesitate in seeking feedback, it's crucial to understand that this effort is not an admission of weakness. Instead, it showcases your dedication to continuous improvement. In your leadership role, where decisions have a significant impact, understanding how you're perceived and how your actions resonate is invaluable.

This is not about changing your core identity, but rather refining how you navigate the intricate landscape of leadership. In a field where strength and resilience are highly regarded, embracing the courage to seek feedback is a strategic move toward enhancing your emotional intelligence and cultivating a more effective leadership style.

Calm Amidst *the* Chaos

The city buzzed with activity as Major Chris Williams strode through the police station corridors, flanked by his trusted companions, Captain Luke Anderson, and Chief Barry Stevens. The air was thick with tension, the recent surge in crime rates and staffing shortages weighing heavily on the minds of the officers. Chris tightened his grip on the stack of reports in his hand, his jaw set with determination.

"I can't believe how bad it's gotten," Captain Anderson muttered, his eyes scanning a crime report. "We've got to do something about this, Major."

Chris nodded, his brow furrowed. "City council is going to try and beat us down. I need you both to back me up in there."

Chief Stevens chimed in, "We're with you, Chris. I'll soften them up and then I'll let you do your thing."

"Why aren't Captain Cipriani and Captain Patterson here for this?" Captain Anderson inquired with genuine curiosity, the question hanging in the air.

"I told them to hang back. They're too busy clashing with each other. I can't risk one of them losing their temper in here," Chief Stevens explained.

As they approached the entrance to the city council meeting room, the trio could feel the gravity of expectations hanging in the air. Stern-faced council members and city officials waited inside, their expressions serious and expectant.

The Chief leaned in before they entered, his voice a low

murmur. "Remember, Chris, we've got your back in there. But they're expecting answers."

"I appreciate that, Chief. Let's get in there and face the storm," Chris replied, taking a deep breath.

The double doors creaked open, revealing the expansive meeting room. Chris took his seat at the table beside Captain Anderson and Chief Stevens. The atmosphere was charged with anticipation as the council members focused their attention on the trio.

City Council President Leanne Bowers leaned forward, her voice laced with skepticism, "Barry, the city is on the brink of erupting with chaos in the streets. People are scared. It seems like you and your team are not equipped to handle this. What's the plan to get things under control? I've got a lot of unanswered questions."

Chief Stevens rose from his seat, his expression resolute. "Ladies and gentlemen of the council, I understand the gravity of the situation. The recent increase in crime is a matter of deep concern to us all. Rest assured, Major Williams and the entire department are taking these challenges seriously."

He paused, emphasizing the weight of his words. "We've been working tirelessly to strategize and implement effective measures to curb this surge. The safety of our citizens remains our top priority, and we are committed to restoring peace to our community."

Chief Stevens gestured toward Chris. "I'll now let Major Williams provide you with a detailed overview of the steps we've taken and the comprehensive plan we have in place. His leadership and dedication to this cause will become evident as he explains the efforts we're undertaking to address these issues head-on."

The chief retook his seat, a sense of confidence in Chris evident in his gaze. The stage was set for him to elaborate on the seriousness of their efforts and reassure the council about the path forward.

Chris felt the collective gaze of the room on him, and a surge of anxiety and uncertainty welled up within him. The pressure was palpable, and the tone of the question presented by the city council president felt like a direct challenge to his capabilities.

Chris stood, acknowledging Chief Stevens with a nod of gratitude, and addressed the council. "Thank you, Chief. As you're aware, the recent uptick in crime has not gone unnoticed within our community. We've identified a significant challenge in fostering effective community engagement, a critical aspect of our crime-fighting strategy."

He continued, his voice unwavering. "To address this, we are allocating additional resources to enhance our presence in the high-crime areas. Community policing initiatives are being revitalized, and we're actively seeking partnerships with local organizations to strengthen our ties with residents."

Chris emphasized the importance of collaboration. "We believe that a united front between law enforcement and the community is key to curbing crime. By increasing our visibility, actively listening to community concerns, and involving residents in the dialogue, we aim to rebuild trust and create a safer environment for all."

As the discussion continued, the questioning intensified. The other city council members probed into specific decisions and resource allocations, each query a subtle jab at Chris' leadership. He felt the heat rising, the massiveness of expectations pressing down on his shoulders.

Captain Luke Anderson, recognizing the escalating tension, interjected, "Major, your thoughts on this matter?"

Chris took a moment to collect himself. The building frustration threatened to spill into his responses, but he was keenly aware of the need to remain composed and be self-aware of the emotions that were building. He could sense those in the room waiting for him to stumble, waiting for a sign of weakness.

"Thank you, Captain," Chris replied to Captain Anderson who sent him a lifeline to pause the barrage of comments, his voice steady. "We value the concerns expressed, and I'm receptive to constructive feedback. As I mentioned earlier, the situation is multifaceted. I don't claim expertise in every aspect, and I welcome any suggestions that could enhance our approach and collaboration with the community."

As the meeting progressed, Chris refrained from responding with defensiveness or anger. Instead, he actively listened to the concerns, acknowledged the validity of some points, and maintained his focus on the larger objective—resolving the challenges facing the city. By the end of the meeting, the intense atmosphere had shifted. Chris' ability to navigate the scrutiny with self-awareness and professionalism left a lasting impression, dispelling some of the doubt that had lingered in the room.

After the meeting, Chris approached Captain Anderson and extended his gratitude, "Thanks for helping me out in there, Luke. I thought they were going to send me outside to the firing squad."

Captain Anderson chuckled, "No need to worry, Major. We're a team. We're navigating some tough waters, but I've got your back."

Chris, visibly relieved, smiled, "I owe you one. This situation has been keeping me up at night."

Captain Anderson patted him on the shoulder, "We'll get through it. Your honesty in the meeting was what made everything go smoothly, and it's a step toward finding solutions that work for everyone. Now go earn that paycheck and figure this out!"

Chris laughed and nodded appreciatively, "Thanks, Luke."

As they parted ways, Chris headed back to his office, reflecting on the challenges ahead and determined to lead his team through the complexities they faced.

Later that evening, as Chris settled into the comforts of his home, Chief Stevens' call interrupted the quiet evening. "Chris, I've been getting positive remarks all night from the city council. Even City Council President Leanne Bowers said she was impressed. I'm pretty sure that's a first for her considering the circumstances."

Chris laughed and humbly acknowledged, "Thank you, Chief. I appreciate the support. I'll see you tomorrow."

Debrief

Meetings with the city council, where the coffee is strong, and the opinions are stronger, can be a minefield for potential blow ups that require a keen awareness of emotional intelligence to avoid.

MEETINGS WITH THE CITY COUNCIL, WHERE THE COFFEE IS STRONG, AND THE OPINIONS ARE STRONGER, CAN BE A MINEFIELD FOR POTENTIAL BLOW UPS THAT REQUIRE A KEEN AWARENESS OF EMOTIONAL INTELLIGENCE TO AVOID

However, Major Chris Williams utilized self-awareness to navigate the intense scrutiny of City Council President Leanne Bowers. As the atmosphere grew tense with concerns about rising crime rates and the overall state of the city, her skeptical inquiry put Chris on the spot, with the entire room observing his response.

Facing the pressure and feeling the density of expectations, Chris initially sensed anxiety and uncertainty welling up within him. However, his self-awareness became evident as he recognized and managed these emotions. Choosing a measured and composed tone, he acknowledged the complexity of the situation and assured the team that active efforts were underway to address the challenges at hand.

Throughout the discussion, as questioning intensified and expectations pressed down on him, Chris strategically maintained his self-awareness. Captain Luke Anderson's intervention provided a momentary respite, and Chris, aware of the escalating tension, took a moment to collect himself. He resisted the temptation to respond with defensiveness or anger, understanding the importance of projecting professionalism. Acknowledging the concerns raised by the city council, Chris actively listened, recognized the validity of some points, and consistently directed the focus towards collaborative problem-solving. By expressing openness to constructive feedback and steering the conversation toward finding collective solutions, he demonstrated a keen awareness of both his own emotions and the dynamics in the room.

By the end of the meeting, Chris's adept use of self-awareness had a transformative effect. The initially skeptical and challenging atmosphere had shifted, and doubts about his leadership had been dispelled. The Major's ability to navigate the situation with poise and professionalism left a lasting impression, instilling confidence in his capacity to lead through challenges.

SECTION 2

Self-Management

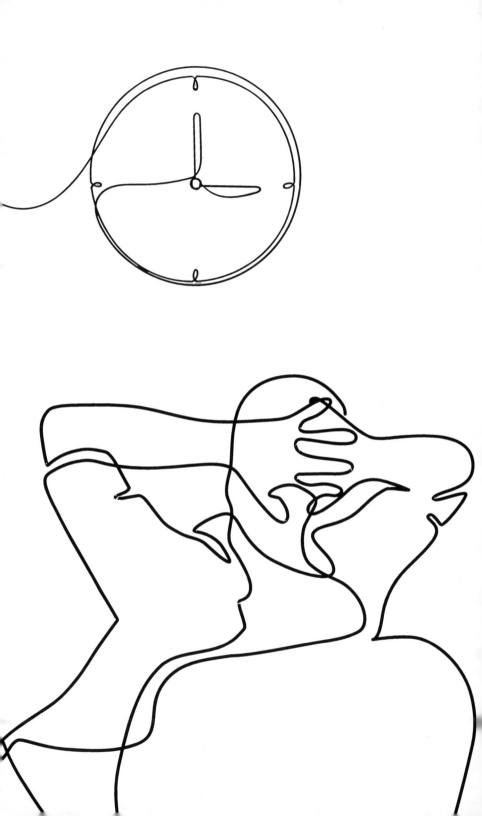

Brewing Discontent

Corporal Frank Martin, a seasoned officer with a grizzled demeanor, grumbled to himself as he navigated his way through the early morning traffic. The sun was barely peeking over the horizon, casting long shadows across the empty streets. Frank couldn't help but feel a sense of annoyance as he made his way to the police station for the dreaded roll call.

On the other end of his Bluetooth headset, Officer Linda Torres listened to Frank's complaints with a patient ear. "I'm telling you, Linda, these roll calls are a waste of time," Frank muttered, his frustration evident in his voice. "Captain's just gonna babble on about some policy changes or community outreach nonsense. We're cops, not social workers."

Linda chuckled on the other end. "Come on, Frank, you know the drill. Gotta keep up appearances and all that. Just nod and pretend to care. Besides, it's not like we have a choice."

As Frank continued his rant, he absentmindedly reached for his cup of coffee in the cup holder. Engrossed in his conversation, he failed to notice the approaching speed bump in the police station parking lot. The coffee cup tipped precariously, and before he could react, a cascade of hot liquid spilled onto his uniform.

"Damn it!" Frank cursed, momentarily losing focus on the road. The spill sent a shock of heat through his body, and he swerved slightly. That distraction proved costly as his car slammed into the speed bump with an unexpected jolt. The sudden impact caused the Bluetooth headset to fly off, leaving Linda's voice echoing through the empty car.

"Frank? Frank, you there?"

Frank, now wide awake and a bit flustered, retrieved the fallen headset and chuckled nervously. "Yeah, Yeah, I'm here. Just hit a damn speed bump. These things are like landmines out here."

"Smooth, real smooth," Linda teased. "Maybe this is a sign, Frank. Pay attention and watch out for those bumps. I'll see you at roll call."

With a sigh, Frank continued toward the station, wiping the spilled coffee off his uniform. As he parked his car and made his way inside, he couldn't shake the feeling that the day was off to a terrible start.

Frank settled into his accustomed spot at the back of the bustling roll call room, his eyes fixed on the clock ticking away on the wall. The room vibrated with the low hum of conversation as officers shuffled in, taking their seats.

As Lieutenant Megan Turner entered the roll call room, Frank observed the weariness in her eyes. Leaning over to Corporal Rachel Buckley, he whispered, "Looks like we're in for a real fun one today," the sarcasm evident in his tone. Just as if she had read his mind, Lieutenant Turner aggressively addressed the room, further dampening Frank's already annoyed mood. The timing couldn't have been worse, as Captain Luke Anderson entered the room.

Captain Anderson, a stern and experienced leader, stepped forward to address the gathered officers.

"Good morning, everyone," Captain Anderson began, his authoritative voice cutting through the room. "I've heard some rumblings about a dip in morale lately, and I want to address it head-on. Policing is tough, and we're facing some serious challenges. Staffing sure isn't helping. But it's crucial that we support each other through thick and thin."

Frank, however, found himself less interested in the captain's words and more irritated by the interruption to his routine. He had a stack of paperwork on his desk and a series of tasks waiting for him, and the captain's message during roll call felt like an unnecessary delay.

As Captain Anderson continued to speak, detailing important information about ongoing cases and upcoming operations, Frank couldn't hide his annoyance. He rolled his eyes, scoffed audibly, and glanced down at his phone with a dismissive demeanor. Unbeknownst to him, the younger officers seated around him were quick to pick up on his disrespectful behavior.

Officer Roberto Rodriguez, a fresh-faced rookie, exchanged puzzled glances with Officer Cliff Jenkins. Their initial enthusiasm for the captain's briefing began to wane as they noticed Frank's lack of interest. The non-verbal cues were contagious, and soon enough, a few other officers followed suit. Whispers and eye rolls from those influenced by Frank spread like wildfire.

Captain Anderson, a perceptive leader, caught wind of the growing unrest. His eyes briefly met Frank's, a silent reprimand passing between them. The captain soldiered on, determined not to let the negativity disrupt the cohesion of the unit, continuing with his usual targeted approach of recognizing officers in the room for a job well done during the previous week.

An hour after the tumultuous roll call concluded, Captain Anderson requested Frank's presence in his office.

"Take a seat, Frank", Captain Anderson said calmly, gesturing to the chair across from his desk. Frank, sensing the mass of the situation, sat down with a serious expression.

"Look, I know roll calls aren't everyone's favorite part of the day," Captain Anderson began, choosing his words carefully. "But we're a team, and we need to present a united front. Our younger officers are looking to us for guidance, and we can't afford to undermine that."

Frank nodded, recognizing the validity of the captain's point. Captain Anderson continued, "I noticed some reactions during roll call today, and it's important that we maintain respect, especially in front of the team. I can't allow that to continue."

Frank sighed, realizing the impact of his actions. "I didn't mean to cause any trouble, Captain. It's just that sometimes these briefings feel like a waste of time when there's so much else to do."

"I understand your concerns," Captain Anderson replied empathetically. "But we can't let our frustrations affect the morale of the team. We need everyone on board, trusting in each other and in our leadership. Your behavior during the roll call sent the wrong message. Those kids look up to you. They are always watching whether you like it or not."

Frank nodded once more, recognizing the seriousness of the situation. Captain Anderson wrapped up, saying, "Frank, let's strive for a balance. I welcome any suggestions you may have to enhance the efficiency of roll calls. Send me your ideas by next week. However," Captain Anderson's tone shifted, compelling Frank to meet his gaze, "ensure that things like this never happen again."

Concluding their conversation, Frank exited the captain's office, having gained a fresh appreciation for Captain Anderson—one that he regretted putting to the test.

Embrace *the* Wave

Life tip: Master the art of self-management. Not every thought needs a parade. It's called an *inner* monologue for a reason – save the fireworks for the grand finale, not the daily show.

Self-management is your ability to regulate and control your emotions, behaviors, and impulses in various situations. It's a crucial facet of emotional intelligence, and, as exemplified by Corporal Frank Martin, the absence of robust self-management skills can compromise your effectiveness and set off an undesirable chain reaction within a police organization.

Building on the foundation of self-awareness, the first pillar of emotional intelligence, self-management takes the insights you've gained about your emotions and uses them to guide your actions and decisions.

Self-awareness involves recognizing and understanding your own emotions, strengths, weaknesses, and values. This awareness is the framework upon which self-management is built. Once you have a clear understanding of your emotional landscape, you can then apply this knowledge to effectively regulate your responses to different stimuli. Self-management involves your ability to stay composed and focused under pressure, adapt to change, and make thoughtful decisions in the face of challenges.

An emotionally intelligent individual with strong self-management skills can navigate a range of situations with grace and resilience. You are less likely to be overwhelmed by stress or succumb to impulsive reactions. Instead, you can channel your emotions in a constructive manner, maintaining a balance between expressing your feelings and exercising control over your responses. This not only contributes to your personal well-being but also fosters positive interactions with others, as individuals with strong self-management skills can create a harmonious and supportive environment.

Once again, Captain Anderson showcased a commendable level of emotional intelligence. He effectively managed his emotions when addressing the situation with Corporal Martin and then skillfully employed the same set of skills to foster a meaningful connection with him.

Self-management serves as the connection between self-awareness and the proficient management of relationships. It empowers you to regulate your emotions, demonstrating adaptability, composure, and a thoughtful approach to decision-making. Self-management is a critical aspect of personal and social success, enabling you to navigate the complexities of human interaction with poise and effectiveness.

Primary Targets
for Self-Management

Breathe

Alright, I understand. The idea of harnessing your breath as a covert weapon for emotional intelligence might elicit quicker eye rolls than a rookie fumbling with handcuffs. But before you dismiss this, hear me out because, surprisingly, there's method to this apparent madness.

In the high-stakes arena of law enforcement, where the unexpected is the only constant, managing emotions is as crucial as knowing where your radio is. Now, I won't ask you to don yoga pants or join a meditation retreat (yet), but I will suggest that your breath can be a surprisingly effective tool in the pursuit of self-awareness and self-management, the first two pillars of emotional intelligence.

Here's the lowdown: when that colleague of yours, the one who has mastered the art of pushing your buttons, starts to irk you, it's time to breathe. It's not about suppressing the irritation or pretending you're in a serene meadow. It's about strategically using your breath to gain control. Inhale deeply, exhale slowly – it's like hitting pause on an emotional rollercoaster.

Why does this work? Well, think of it as a tactical move. By taking that conscious breath, you create a brief moment for self-reflection. It's a mini time-out, allowing you to assess your emotions, recognize any triggers, and respond with a level head instead of reacting in the heat of the moment.

Keep in mind that emotions themselves are neither positive nor negative - they simply exist. Yet, the significance lies in how you respond to them.

No one must be aware that a particular lieutenant irks you. Rest assured, others likely share the sentiment. Your responsibility is to acknowledge that emotion, take a breath, and respond thoughtfully instead of reacting impulsively. This is the essence of emotional intelligence.

KEEP IN MIND THAT EMOTIONS THEMSELVES ARE NEITHER POSITIVE NOR NEGATIVE—THEY SIMPLY EXIST.

Now, for the skeptics in the room, here's a practical tidbit: when annoyance creeps in, try the 4-7-8 technique. Inhale for a count of 4, hold your breath for 7, and exhale for 8. It's like a quick reset button for your nervous system. Or, if you're feeling a bit rebellious, go for the "square breathing" method—inhale for 4 counts, hold for 4, exhale for 4, and hold for 4 again. It's like creating a Zen square in the midst of chaos.

So, the next time you find yourself on the brink of an eyeroll at the mention of using your breath, consider it a tool in your emotional intelligence toolkit.

Get Moving

The only acceptable elephant in the room is the one you're trying to mimic in your yoga class, not the one representing your ignored gym membership.

I understand. Being a leader is more about navigating through bureaucratic mazes than running laps around the station. And who needs a gym membership when you've got the heart-pounding adrenaline rush of decoding department policies? But there comes a moment when even the most seasoned coffee mug needs a workout buddy – and that workout buddy is none other than exercise.

Rest assured, for those of you tirelessly patrolling the streets day in and day out, this is not a message exclusively tailored for your desk-bound comrades. Your relentless dedication to street duty hasn't escaped notice, and let it be known that the prescription for exercise is as much a daily imperative for you as it is for your office-dwelling counterparts. Whether you're chasing down leads or clocking in the miles on the beat, consider this a friendly nudge to incorporate physical activity into your routine.

In the journey of law enforcement, particularly when leading a team, the commitment to service often comes with sacrifices. One of those sacrifices, though not often spoken about, is the demand on your physical well-being. It's entirely possible that nobody mentioned this, especially when you step into a leadership role—but you've essentially forfeited the luxury of not maintaining a reasonable standard of fitness. It's not just about the uniform. It's about embodying the resilience and discipline that the badge symbolizes.

IT'S ENTIRELY POSSIBLE THAT NOBODY MENTIONED THIS, ESPECIALLY WHEN YOU STEP INTO A LEADERSHIP ROLE—BUT YOU'VE ESSENTIALLY FORFEITED THE LUXURY OF NOT MAINTAINING A REASONABLE STANDARD OF FITNESS

Building on the importance of intentional breathing in self-management, let's explore the practicality of incorporating exercise into your life. The daily grind of leadership doesn't always leave room for lengthy gym sessions or marathon runs. But here's the reality check – staying in shape doesn't demand an all-or-nothing approach. It demands something, anything, that keeps your body moving and your mind refreshed.

Exercise becomes the anchor that connects you with your commitment to service. It's not about sculpting the perfect physique. It's about ensuring that the physical vessel you inhabit is up to the challenges you face daily. Whether it's a brisk walk, a quick workout routine, or a commitment to take the stairs instead of the elevator, these small actions are declarations. They declare that you recognize the weight of responsibility that comes with the badge, and you're actively doing something about it.

Consider the daily workout, not as an obligation, but as a deposit into your own physical and mental well-being account. A jog around the block or a few sets of bodyweight exercises can be as powerful for the mind as it is for the body. The routine doesn't have to be monotonous, it just has to be consistent. It's a commitment to yourself, your team, and the community you serve.

In this dance of self-management, exercise becomes the partner that keeps you agile, both physically and mentally. This is about demonstrating to your team that the commitment to service starts with yourself. So, let's lace up those sneakers not out of vanity but out of a profound dedication to being the leaders our community deserves.

Spring Cleaning

Leading without organization is like trying to navigate a maze blindfolded—it might be an adventure, but chances are you'll bump into more problems than solutions. In a world where unpredictability is the only certainty, effective organization becomes a crucial tool for you as you continue down the path of enhancing your self-management skills and, consequently, elevating your emotional intelligence. The demanding nature of your job, coupled with the ever-present potential for high-stress situations, underscores the need for you to navigate your responsibilities with a strategic and monitored approach. Put simply, organization is essential.

A hallmark of self-management is your ability to regulate your emotions and responses effectively. Constant stress, often exacerbated by disorganization and poor time management, can significantly hinder this regulatory capacity. When you find yourself drowning in a sea of tasks, deadlines, and operational demands, the stressors accumulate, potentially leading to emotional exhaustion and diminished decision-making capabilities.

CONSTANT STRESS, OFTEN EXACERBATED BY DISORGANIZATION AND POOR TIME MANAGEMENT, CAN SIGNIFICANTLY HINDER YOUR ABILITY TO PRACTICE SELF-MANAGEMENT EFFECTIVELY.

Effective organization will allow you to establish priorities, allocate resources efficiently, and maintain a structured approach to your responsibilities. By implementing strategic planning and organizational systems, you can create a work environment that minimizes unnecessary stressors, providing you with the mental bandwidth to navigate challenges with composure and clarity.

Consider a scenario where you are in a leadership role, overwhelmed by administrative tasks and operational demands, consistently feeling the inertia of impending deadlines. This constant pressure not only impedes your ability to make sound decisions but also takes a toll on your overall well-being. However, with effective time management and organization practices, including setting realistic goals, breaking down tasks into manageable steps, and utilizing scheduling tools, you can regain a sense of control over your workload.

A well-organized approach, however, requires a proactive rather than reactive mindset. You can allocate dedicated time for critical tasks, strategic planning, and personal well-being, creating a buffer against the chaos of unexpected events. This proactive stance not only enhances self-management but also contributes to a more resilient and emotionally intelligent leadership style.

Overall, it's crucial to recognize the vital connection between effective time management, organization, and self-management. The ability to organize tasks, prioritize responsibilities, and navigate daily challenges with a structured approach not only alleviates chronic stress but also lays the footing for heightened emotional intelligence. By mastering the art of time management, you can create a more conducive environment for self-management, ultimately fostering a leadership style characterized by resilience, adaptability, and emotional composure in the face of adversity.

Discipline

Let us playfully imagine that Jocko Willink moonlights as the unofficial godfather of discipline in your universe. While he might not have a trademark on the concept, he certainly embodies the ethos of getting things done with unwavering commitment.

For those not acquainted with Jocko Willink, picture him as the unsung hero of discipline in your professional lives. A former Navy SEAL turned leadership guru, Jocko embodies the ethos of getting things done with unwavering commitment. You can find him sharing his insights on discipline and leadership in his books like *Extreme Ownership* or on his popular podcast, *The Jocko Podcast*.

Discipline isn't just a buzzword. It's the secret sauce for cultivating self-management and fortifying your emotional intelligence.

When it comes to navigating the intricacies of leadership, especially in managing meetings, making crucial decisions, or balancing personal matters, discipline takes center stage. It's the steady hand that guides you through the daily hustle, ensuring you maintain composure when faced with challenges. Discipline becomes particularly apparent in those moments when the temptation to procrastinate is high, and yet, you choose to tackle tasks head-on, building resilience in the process.

DISCIPLINE BECOMES PARTICULARLY APPARENT IN THOSE MOMENTS WHEN THE TEMPTATION TO PROCRASTINATE IS HIGH, AND YET, YOU CHOOSE TO TACKLE TASKS HEAD-ON, BUILDING RESILIENCE IN THE PROCESS.

In the arena of self-management, discipline translates into making intentional choices that align with your emotional well-being. It's about staying focused on your goals, even when distractions abound. For police leaders, discipline means showing up for your teams with a clear mind, ready to handle the emotional complexities of the job. It's the commitment to regular self-reflection, acknowledging your strengths and areas for growth.

Building emotional intelligence requires discipline in recognizing and regulating your own emotions. It's about approaching situations with a level head, making decisions based on reason rather than reactive impulses. Discipline manifests in the conscious effort to understand your own emotions so you can then be more in-tune with the emotions of those around you, fostering a culture of empathy within your teams.

So, here's to embracing discipline not just as a tool for ticking off tasks but as a guiding force in your journey of self-management and the cultivation of emotional intelligence. It's the subtle art of choosing responses over reactions, fostering a leadership style that resonates with both strength and compassion.

Mayhem Mastery

Lieutenant Jessica Hayes intently watched the winding road in front of her, tension evident in her furrowed brow as she sped through the city streets. The echo of the police radio rippled through the squad car, a constant reminder of the chaos awaiting her at the stabbing scene.

Jessica cleared her mind, toggling the mic button on the radio. "Dispatch, this is Lieutenant Hayes. I'm en route to the stabbing. What's the status on that perimeter?"

"Lieutenant, we've got units trying, but it's a mess. Sounds like a lot of people leaving the area", echoed the dispatcher.

Jessica clenched her jaw, frustration building. "Copy, Dispatch. I want additional units to seal off all exits. No one in or out until we've got control."

"10-4, Lieutenant", the dispatcher confirmed.

Jessica's gaze darted between the road and the radio, her mind racing through the checklist of tasks that should be happening. However, silence laced the air waves.

She pressed the mic again. "And where's the information on the suspects? We need that out over the air."

"Working on it, Lieutenant", the dispatcher anxiously responded.

Jessica took a deep breath, her tone stern. "Show me out on scene."

The night hung heavy as Jessica arrived at the crime scene. The chilling sight of flashing lights and uniformed officers sig-

naled an investigation in progress. Sergeant Curtis Lockley, who was tasked with briefing her, appeared visibly frazzled as he rushed toward her.

"Lieutenant, we've got a stabbing. Victim's over there, and we're still securing the area," he stammered, handing her a folder with sparse details.

Jessica scanned the hastily compiled information, frustration bubbling within her as she noted the lack of coherence. "Curtis, what is this? I need accurate details. What happened here? Do we have any witnesses, suspects, or evidence that needs to be locked down? What about the perimeter?"

Sergeant Lockley fumbled with his words. "Well, the initial report says the victim was attacked, but, um, we haven't identified any witnesses yet. The scene is still, uh, not contained."

Jessica's patience wore thin, but she recognized the need for control. The lack of containment and the absence of crucial details set off alarms in her mind. "Sergeant, we can't afford to let the scene remain uncontained. I need you to coordinate with the officers on the perimeter and make sure no one leaves. We could be losing valuable witnesses right now."

As she spoke, Jessica saw witnesses drifting away, their potential information slipping through the night. Suppressing her frustration, she continued, "Find out who our witnesses are and hold on to them until detectives arrive. And make sure the scene is properly secured. We can't afford to get sloppy here."

Sergeant Lockley nodded, understanding the urgency in the lieutenant's voice. He hurried to carry out her instructions, and Jessica took a moment to collect herself. The adrenaline of the situation, coupled with the sergeant's disarray, threatened to ignite her temper. However, she knew that losing her cool wouldn't rectify the situation.

As Jessica worked to bring order to the chaotic scene, she couldn't help but notice the younger officers, still uncertain and frazzled. Their faces reflected the gravity of the situation, and the lack of clear direction had left them unsure of their roles.

Addressing the officers closest to her, Jessica detailed, "I know this is a tense situation, but we need to focus. We're a team, and we've got a job to do. Secure the perimeter, identify witnesses, and don't move any evidence you find. Let's work together and keep this scene under control."

The younger officers, seeking guidance, looked to Jessica for reassurance. Her calm but firm tone helped steady their nerves, and they began to organize themselves more effectively. As the perimeter tightened and witnesses were identified, the scene gained a semblance of order.

Approaching a recently onboarded officer who appeared somewhat flustered, Jessica warmly inquired, "How are you holding up, Harris?"

Officer Wayne Harris, still a bit uncertain, responded, "Uh, just fine, ma'am."

"Harris, pause for a moment. You're doing fine. Go help with securing the perimeter on that side of the scene. If you come across any witnesses, gather their information, and let Sergeant Lockley know when you cross paths with him. We're in good shape," she stated with a firmness that Officer Harris desperately needed. Officer Harris nodded, visibly relieved to have a specific task.

As Jessica moved through the scene, she repeated similar instructions to other officers, providing them with clear roles to play. The lieutenant's self-awareness allowed her to empathize with the overwhelming nature of the situation for these officers, and her self-management ensured that her guidance was delivered with the necessary composure.

As the team moved into action, Jessica monitored the progress, her self-awareness guiding her responses. She approached witnesses with a calm but assertive demeanor. Meanwhile, Sergeant Lockley reorganized the perimeter, ensuring that no potential witnesses escaped.

Sergeant Lockley, having regrouped with more accurate information, approached Jessica. "Lieutenant, the perimeter is secure, and we have all of the witnesses ready for detectives when they get here. EMS is on standby for any potential medical assistance. What's our next move?"

"Good work, Sarge. Let's coordinate with the detectives when they get here. Check any available surveillance footage from nearby businesses and homes. We can't afford to let any leads slip through the cracks," Jessica responded, her focus shifting to the next phase of the investigation.

As the night unfolded, the scene transformed from chaos to controlled diligence. The younger officers, once frazzled, began to find their footing under Jessica's clear direction. The stabbing investigation progressed methodically, each officer contributing to the collective effort. During a challenging situation, Jessica had exemplified not only effective leadership but also the importance of self-awareness and self-management while navigating the complexities of the scene.

In the aftermath, as the investigation progressed, Jessica took a moment to privately address the frazzled sergeant. "Curtis, listen. In these situations, clear communication is key. We can't afford confusion. I need you to stay focused, give me accurate information, and ensure our procedures are followed. You have to set a good example for these guys out here."

Sergeant Lockley nodded, his expression a mix of acknowledgment and remorse. "I understand, Lieutenant. It won't happen again. I'll make sure to keep things tight and communicate more effectively."

Jessica placed a reassuring hand on his shoulder. "I know you can, Curtis. We're a team, and I need you at your best. Now, let's focus on getting everyone out of here on time."

Later that night, Jessica found herself driving back to headquarters, the red and blue hues of police lights fading in the rearview mirror. The magnitude of the investigation dwelled on her mind, but she knew there was one more important task to attend to.

The phone rang, and she observed her husband's name lighting up the screen, a sure sign that her son, Mason, was on the line to wish her goodnight.

"Hey, sweetie," she answered with a smile, trying to shift her focus from the grim scene to the warmth of her family.

"Hi, Mommy! Are you still at work?" her son asked, his voice filled with innocence.

"Yeah, I am, but I'll be home soon. Did you brush your teeth and get ready for bed?" Jessica inquired, seamlessly switching gears from a stern investigator to a caring mother.

"Uh-huh! Can you read me a story when you get home?" he asked, his excitement palpable.

"Of course, I will. Now, it's time for you to go to sleep. I love you, sweetheart," Jessica said, her heart swelling with love.

"I love you too, Mommy! Goodnight!" he exclaimed before ending the call.

Jessica sighed, the pressure of the investigation momentarily lifted by the love and innocence of her son. As she drove through the quiet streets, she couldn't help but reflect on the delicate balance she maintained between her duty as a lieutenant and her role as a mother. The night held both darkness and warmth, a stark reminder of the complexities of life and the constant juggling act required to navigate it.

Debrief

Lieutenant Jessica Hayes exhibited remarkable self-management skills during a challenging stabbing investigation. Confronted with incomplete information and a visibly frazzled sergeant, Jessica, though annoyed and angry, demonstrated self-awareness by recognizing her emotions. Despite the pressure, she maintained composure and issued clear directives to urgently address the situation, emphasizing the need for proper coordination and containment.

Jessica's ability to manage her emotions was crucial in navigating the high-pressure scenario. Despite the initial frustration, she actively engaged with the team, assigning specific tasks to junior officers, and fostering a collaborative and organized response. Her calm and assertive demeanor helped steady the nerves of the team and instilled confidence in their collective efforts.

As Jessica moved through the investigation, her self-awareness remained evident. While interacting with witnesses and monitoring progress, she acknowledged her initial annoyance and anger but channelized these emotions into effective leadership. Her measured approach with Sergeant Lockley in the aftermath showcased her commitment to improvement, emphasizing the critical importance of clear communication.

Jessica not only exemplified effective leadership during the investigation but also showcased her profound ability to switch gears when her son, Mason, called to say goodnight. Despite experiencing annoyance and anger earlier in the evening, she skillfully navigated the situation, ensuring her son was not impacted by what she had just experienced.

SECTION 3

Social Awareness

An Unspoken Battle

Sergeant Mark Roberts sat at his desk, the dim light casting shadows on the worn-out papers scattered in front of him. His mind, however, was far from focused on his role as a leader. The furrowed lines on his forehead deepened as he mulled over the daunting prospect of paying for his son's college education.

"Damn tuition fees," he muttered under his breath, his eyes fixed on the financial documents spread out before him. The numbers seemed to dance, mocking him with their relentless demands. His son's dreams were on the line, and he felt the weight of that responsibility pressing down on him.

A quick glance at the clock jolted him back to the present. He sighed, realizing he was running out of time. Picking up the phone, he dialed his ex-wife's number. The conversation was brief, but the tension in his voice betrayed the internal struggle he was facing.

"I'll be there as soon as I can," he assured, ending the call with a heavy exhale. He knew he was going to be late picking up his son again. The guilt gnawed at him, but the pressing matters at hand seemed to overshadow everything.

The dimly lit conference room sizzled with anticipation as the detectives took their seats. Mark stood at the front, his slumped posture and stained tie narrating a tale more profound than any words could convey.

A cloud of tension hung in the air, and the source was Detective Sydney Jacobs, a seasoned investigator with a wealth of experience. Mark, engrossed in his own thoughts, barely acknowledged the undercurrents in the room. The heaviness of his own concerns had blinded him to the subtle cues of discontent playing out among his detectives.

"As you all know, City Council President Leanne Bowers wants answers for the shooting last weekend. Jacobs, what's the deal with this. We can't take lightly having the city council president's son as a person of interest in a shooting investigation," Mark declared, his mind preoccupied with his own troubles.

Detective Jacobs, growing increasingly frustrated, exchanged glances with her colleagues. She raised her hand, hoping to address the deeper issues at play.

"Sarge, we've been grappling with this case all week. We need a strategic plan, we are running in circles over here," Detective Jacobs suggested, trying to steer the conversation toward a more comprehensive solution.

Mark, however, was too wrapped up in his own concerns to appreciate the subtleties of Detective Jacob's plea. Dismissing it with a wave, he snapped, "We don't have time for grand plans, Jacobs. I look like a fool every time I have to brief the lieutenant on this. It doesn't help that I have Captain Cipriani and Captain Patterson in my ear too."

The seasoned detective sighed, glancing at her fellow investigators, who mirrored her frustration. Detective George Ramirez, a younger member of the team, spoke up tentatively, "Sarge, maybe we could brainstorm together, we could use the help."

Mark, his patience worn thin, retorted, "We don't need group therapy, Ramirez. We need results. And we need them now."

The meeting continued, with Mark oblivious to the growing rift in the room. As the officers filed out, Detective Jacobs caught up with the younger Detective Ramirez.

"Thanks man, I appreciate your attempt to get through to him in there, but sometimes the higher-ups just won't listen," Detective Jacobs said, a hint of resignation in her voice.

Back at his desk, Mark buried himself in paperwork, oblivious to the uneasy atmosphere he had left behind. Detective Jacobs, frustrated and feeling unheard, shared a knowing look with Detective Ramirez, a silent acknowledgment of the challenges they faced under a leader too consumed by his own struggles to see the fractures forming within the team.

Mark pulled up in front of his ex-wife's house, the engine idling as he waited for his son to emerge. The door opened, and a tired-looking teenager slumped into the passenger seat.

"Hey, Dad," the boy mumbled, avoiding eye contact.

"Hey, champ," Mark replied absentmindedly, his mind still tethered to the lingering issues at work. He glanced at his son, taking note of the fatigue etched across his face. "Long day?"

His son merely nodded, gazing out of the window. The car started moving, and a heavy silence settled between them.

Mark's thoughts remained anchored to the workload awaiting him at the office the next day. "How's everything at your mom's place?"

"Fine," came the curt response.

The streetlights flickered as they drove through the quiet

neighborhood. Mark stole glances at his son, grappling with the right words to bridge the growing gap, but his mind kept drifting back to work.

"You know, if there's anything on your mind, you can always talk to me," Mark offered, his eyes focused on the road.

His son rolled his eyes, frustration evident in his voice. "Yeah, Dad, if you'd actually listen."

Mark's attention snapped back, realizing the disconnect. "Sorry, what was that?"

"Never mind," the boy muttered, crossing his arms, and turning away. The rest of the drive home unfolded in strained silence, the force of unspoken thoughts hanging in the air.

Room Reconnaissance

If you're stuck in your own self-sabotage, you're likely missing out on what's right in front of you. Clear the fog, and you might be surprised at the opportunities that have been there all along.

Social awareness is a key component of emotional intelligence, involving your ability to perceive, understand, and navigate the emotions of others in various social situations. It means being attuned to the feelings, needs, and perspectives of those around you, fostering empathy and effective interpersonal relationships. This skill enables you to interpret nonverbal cues, such as body language and facial expressions, as well as the spoken words of others. Social awareness goes beyond simple observation. It involves recognizing the underlying emotions that may not be explicitly expressed.

Let's consider Sergeant Mark Roberts' situation as a stark illustration of the consequences that can arise when individuals lack self-awareness and struggle with self-management, leaving social awareness off the menu. In the context of emotional intelligence, self-awareness is the base layer that allows you to recognize and understand your own emotions, strengths, and limitations. Without this foundational awareness, individuals like Sergeant Roberts may find themselves blindsided by personal challenges, which, in turn, hampers their ability to effectively navigate social situations.

BUILDING UPON THE FOUNDATION OF SELF-AWARENESS AND SELF-MANAGEMENT, SOCIAL AWARENESS IS AN EXTENSION OF YOUR UNDERSTANDING OF YOUR OWN EMOTIONS AND THE ABILITY TO REGULATE THEM.

Building upon the infrastructure of self-awareness and self-management, social awareness is an extension of your understanding of your own emotions and the ability to regulate them. Social awareness directs your attention outward, acknowledging that emotions are a shared and influential aspect of human interaction. It involves your capacity to recognize the emotional states of others, comprehend their perspectives, and respond with sensitivity. Through social awareness, you can cultivate better communication, build stronger connections, and foster a positive and supportive social environment. It also involves understanding the dynamics of groups, adapting to diverse social situations, and being cognizant of the broader emotional climate in a given context.

At its core, social awareness elevates emotional intelligence by shifting the focus beyond individual emotions to encompass the emotional experiences of others. This encourages a holistic understanding of human emotions, fostering deeper connections, effective collaboration, and adept maneuvering through the complexities of social interactions. Nurturing social awareness is an ongoing process that demands your active listening, openness, and a genuine curiosity about the emotions and perspectives of those with whom you interact.

Primary Targets
for Social Awareness

Just Listen

Hit the pause button on that hamster wheel for a sec, and you might actually pick up on some sage advice. Turns out, the hamster has more than just a spin cycle—it's got a wisdom wheel too.

Active and attentive listening is a crucial skill for enhancing your social awareness and developing emotional intelligence. Often, you engage in conversations with the primary goal of expressing your thoughts and opinions, neglecting the fundamental aspect of genuinely hearing what others have to say. In both personal and professional contexts, mastering the art of listening can significantly improve your relationships and contribute to effective communication.

For you, honing this skill is particularly vital, as it can enhance your ability to connect with your team members, the community, and other stakeholders. One way to improve active listening is by consciously focusing on the speaker and resisting the temptation to formulate a response while they are talking. Instead of mentally preparing counterarguments or solutions, you should give your full attention to the speaker, making eye contact and nodding to indicate understanding.

ONE WAY TO IMPROVE ACTIVE LISTENING IS BY CONSCIOUSLY FOCUSING ON THE SPEAKER AND RESISTING THE TEMPTATION TO FORMULATE A RESPONSE WHILE THEY ARE TALKING.

Additionally, paraphrasing what the speaker has shared can be a powerful technique. This involves summarizing the speaker's words in your own language to confirm understanding and show that their perspective is valued. For instance, if a community member is expressing concerns about safety in a particular neighborhood, you might respond by saying, "It sounds like you're worried about the recent increase in crime, and you'd like to see more police presence in the area. Is that correct?" This not only demonstrates active listening but also conveys empathy and a genuine desire to understand the concerns of the community.

Fostering an open and inclusive environment encourages effective communication. You can create opportunities for your team members to share their thoughts and concerns without fear of judgment. Regular team meetings and one-on-one check-ins are examples of initiatives that promote open dialogue. By actively engaging with your team and community, you can build trust, improve your social awareness, and demonstrate a commitment to emotional intelligence.

Step Back And Watch

Remember our previous conversation about cultivating self-awareness by adopting a detective's mindset to recognize your personal triggers and emotions? Get ready to stroll through a similar expedition aimed at boosting your social awareness.

Picture this: imagine yourself donning a metaphorical detective hat, not to solve a crime, but to unravel the subtle mysteries of human interaction. To truly excel in your role, you must step out of your own head and embrace a Sherlock Holmes mindset, complete with a magnifying glass for scrutinizing the intricate details of social dynamics.

One essential tool in your detective kit is the ability to observe the room with a watchful eye. Instead of being lost in the labyrinth of your own thoughts, you can benefit from taking a step back to survey the scene. It's like playing a strategic game of chess, but with people. Who is huddled in intense conversation, and who is subtly signaling for assistance? The room becomes a canvas, and you, as the astute leader, are the painter, creating a mental masterpiece of social connections and cues.

Think of yourself as a social Sherlock, sporting a metaphorical monocle and a pipe. Instead of searching for fingerprints, you're on the lookout for subtle clues in body language and non-verbal cues. Step into the world of Body Language 101 – where every gesture is a clue, and understanding the social code is the key.

In this whimsical quest for social mastery, you can transform your approach, creating an environment where communication is not just about words but about the unspoken language that binds a team.

The clues to effective leadership may just be hiding in the nuances of the room around you.

INSTEAD OF BEING LOST IN THE LABYRINTH OF YOUR OWN THOUGHTS, YOU CAN BENEFIT FROM TAKING A STEP BACK TO SURVEY THE SCENE.

Be Social

Consider this your official invitation to venture beyond the screen, the desk, wherever you find comfort, and engage in the ancient art of conversation. Yes, I'm suggesting you talk to actual people.

In the hierarchical structure of law enforcement, you will often find yourself navigating complex responsibilities, sometimes inadvertently isolating yourself from the day-to-day experiences of the rank and file. This detachment can impede the development of your emotional intelligence, particularly around social awareness. To enhance this crucial aspect of your leadership, you must deliberately break free from the isolation and actively engage with your teams.

In other words, it might be time for you to trade in your solitude for some socialization.

One effective strategy for you to improve social awareness is to prioritize regular and meaningful interactions with officers at all levels. This involves more than scheduled briefings. It requires informal engagements where you can connect on a personal level. Participating in roll calls, attending shift briefings, and even sharing a casual conversation in common areas can provide valuable insights into the challenges and emotions experienced by frontline officers.

Getting to know officer's names serves as a fantastic initial step toward becoming more sociable and encouraging individuals to share a bit more as you expand your social horizons. We'll take a closer look at this leadership insight in a moment. Hang tight.

Also, fostering an open-door policy encourages officers to approach you with their concerns and perspectives. This accessibility not only breaks down barriers but also signals to the rank and file that their voices are valued. By actively seeking out diverse viewpoints within the force, you can broaden your understanding of the emotional landscape, identify potential sources of stress, and address issues before they escalate.

Get ready for this nugget of wisdom: cultivating humility is equally essential when striving for enhanced social awareness.

GET READY FOR THIS NUGGET OF WISDOM: CULTIVATING HUMILITY IS EQUALLY ESSENTIAL WHEN STRIVING FOR ENHANCED SOCIAL AWARENESS.

Acknowledging that leadership does not equate to having all the answers allows you to learn from your teams. This humility creates an environment where open communication is encouraged, and you can absorb valuable insights from those with firsthand experiences in the field.

You must recognize the potential isolation that comes with your role and actively work to counteract it to enhance social awareness. I understand that it might feel awkward initially. However, once officers become familiar with you and realize your positive intentions, having a supervisor engaged in a conversation with a group of young officers won't appear as a stern directive but rather as a regular, everyday interaction.

Exchange Perspectives

Picture asking for feedback on what you are seeing like tossing a line into the opinion pond. At times, you snag a big catch, but occasionally, you might find unexpected surprises—like your complete lack of social awareness. But hey, the journey is always an adventure!

The road to enhancing your social awareness as part of a broader effort to improve your emotional intelligence is a commendable endeavor. However, the path to heightened social acuity should not be a solitary one. Engage in open and constructive discussions with others to significantly amplify your learning process, serving as a valuable mirror reflecting the nuances of your social interactions.

Steer clear of turning this collaborative effort into a gossip extravaganza – we know how notorious the law enforcement culture can be for swapping stories. Instead, focus on sharing observations and insights to elevate your social awareness game and decode those elusive social cues. Sharing observations with trusted colleagues or mentors creates a collaborative space for reflection.

STEER CLEAR OF TURNING THIS COLLABORATIVE EFFORT INTO A GOSSIP EXTRAVAGANZA – WE KNOW HOW NOTORIOUS THE LAW ENFORCEMENT CULTURE CAN BE FOR SWAPPING STORIES

Through these discussions, you can gain valuable perspectives on your own social awareness. Are there subtle cues being missed? Are there patterns of behavior that go unnoticed? These conversations not only enrich your own awareness but also contribute to a collective learning experience, fostering a culture of continuous improvement within our team or organization. Discussing observations with others provides an opportunity to validate perceptions.

Social dynamics can be complex and nuanced, and what you interpret as a specific cue might be viewed differently by another. By engaging in open conversations, you can cross-reference your observations, identifying commonalities and disparities. This collaborative approach acts as a checks-and-balances system, refining and honing the accuracy of social awareness.

These discussions should be framed in a positive and growth-oriented manner. Rather than focusing on criticizing or pointing out flaws, the aim is to collectively elevate the team's emotional intelligence. Encouraging a culture of open communication and feedback allows individuals to share their insights without fear of judgment, fostering an environment conducive to self-improvement. Engaging in thoughtful discussions with others provides a valuable support system for refining your understanding of social cues, validating observations, and fostering a culture of continuous learning. It transforms the journey towards heightened emotional intelligence into a shared expedition, where each participant contributes to the collective growth of our team.

Unity In Turbulence

The morning had unfolded like a slow burn in Chief Barry Stevens' office. Tensions simmered beneath the surface as Captain Andrea Cipriani and Captain Jim Patterson engaged in a heated argument, their voices rising and falling in a discordant symphony of disagreement.

The city and the police department found themselves in a tense situation following a shooting investigation from the previous weekend, which implicated the son of City Council President Leanne Bowers. While Chief Steven's meeting with the city council went well earlier in the day, the heat was still on.

As the door closed behind Detective Sydney Jacobs, who had just left the room after a tense exchange with the captains, the atmosphere grew heavy with unspoken animosity. Barry, seated behind his desk, steepled his fingers and leaned forward, trying to maintain control of the escalating situation.

"You can't keep going behind my back and telling my people what to do, Andrea!" Captain Patterson's voice sliced through the air, frustration evident in every word.

Captain Cipriani, her face flushed with anger, retorted, "You're not getting things done. I know what I'm doing, this thing is going to hit the news and we must get ahead of it!"

The room crackled with the intensity of their disagreement, the echoes of their argument reverberating off the walls. As the captains traded accusations and grievances, the underlying issue became clear—it was a clash of methodologies and egos, each captain staunchly defending their approach to the investigation.

Barry, known for his measured demeanor, struggled to mediate. "Listen, you two need to find a way to work together. I'm not going to let you both bring this ship down because you can't play nice."

Captain Patterson, his jaw clenched, shot back, "Play nice? It's hard to play nice when one side constantly undermines the other."

Captain Cipriani's response was equally biting, "Undermines or actually gets things done? There's a difference, Patterson."

The tension in the room reached its peak, the air thick with unresolved conflict. Both captains stood on opposite sides of the chief's desk, their gazes locked in a battle of wills.

Barry knew that the discord between these two key figures could jeopardize the entire investigation. As the captains left the room, the weight of their unspoken disagreements lingered.

Barry paced in his office, a storm brewing in his eyes. He glanced at the clock, recognizing the imminent press conference. The strained relationships among the captains weighed heavily on him.

The press conference room hummed with anticipation as Barry approached the podium. Reporters poised with their cameras, ready to capture every word. Barry took a moment to survey the room, recognizing the tension in the air and the expectant gazes of his officers. His internal dialogue swirled with awareness, knowing that his every word would shape the narrative.

"Good afternoon, everyone. I know you're all eager for an update on the recent developments, and I appreciate your patience," Barry began, his voice steady. As he spoke, he noticed a collective shift in body language—a subtle but palpable increase in anxiety. A reporter shouted, "Chief, is it true there's been a setback in the investigation?"

Barry's mind raced as he picked up on the heightened anticipation. He took a deep breath, deciding to address the question head-on. "Yes, we've faced some challenges, but setbacks are a part of any complex investigation. I want to assure the public and our dedicated officers that we are committed to finding the truth and bringing justice to those affected."

A reporter pressed, "Chief, how do you respond to rumors about internal conflicts within the department hindering the investigation?" The room held its breath.

Barry acknowledged the potential damage that such rumors could inflict on the morale of his team, pondering how news of internal discord among his staff had spread so rapidly. He chose his words carefully, "In any large organization, differences of opinion may arise. However, I can assure you that our focus remains on the investigation, and we are working collaboratively to resolve this case."

Then, the chief, keenly aware of the internal conflicts within the department, turned his attention to his staff members in the room, including Captain Patterson and Captain Cipriani. With a subtle look and a reassuring nod, he silently conveyed a message of unity. Despite their differences, they were a team. The unspoken gesture, a shared understanding among the staff members and officers present in the room, provided a sense of stability amid the challenges they faced.

As the questions continued, Barry's internal radar remained

active. Detective Sydney Jacobs, a key member of the investigative team who had briefly witnessed the argument between the captains earlier, looked visibly tense. Barry caught her eye and gave a subtle nod, acknowledging the pressure the detective was under.

A reporter, known for their persistence, pressed, "Chief, can you explain why no arrests have been made yet? The public is growing impatient."

The question added another layer of complexity to an already challenging situation. Barry felt the pressure of the public's expectations. His internal dialogue urged caution, "I need to address this with transparency, but also manage expectations." He responded, "I understand the public's concern, and we share their urgency. However, in complex investigations, arrests must be based on solid evidence. We are diligently working to gather the necessary information to ensure a thorough and just resolution."

After the press conference, Barry closed the door to his office, acknowledging the heightened scrutiny. He contemplated the delicate balance between transparency and maintaining public trust. He called Detective Sydney Jacobs in, saying, "Sydney, I regret that you had to witness that brief disagreement earlier," a touch of embarrassment evident in his tone. "Rest assured, I have your back and I will see this through to the end with you."

Detective Jacobs, visibly relieved, responded, "Thank you, Chief. It's been tough, but knowing we have your support means a lot."

Debrief

Chief Barry Stevens exhibited a masterful blend of self-awareness, self-management, and social awareness as he navigated a challenging press conference and internal conflict within his staff. Aware of the tension in the room and the expectations placed on him, he began with a measured acknowledgment of the audience's eagerness for updates. As reporters posed probing questions, Barry recognized the rising anxiety in the room and skillfully managed his own emotions, responding with composure and transparency.

In the face of a pointed question about setbacks and internal conflicts, Barry leveraged self-management to address the concerns head-on, reassuring the public and emphasizing the department's commitment to collaboration. His careful choice of words aimed at maintaining public trust showcased his awareness of the potential impact of rumors on team morale.

Barry's social awareness also came into play during the press conference, extending beyond verbal communication. A subtle look and reassuring nod toward his staff conveyed a powerful message of unity, fostering stability amid internal conflicts. Recognizing Detective Jacobs' visible tension, Barry acknowledged the pressure and silently communicated support, demonstrating an acute awareness of his team's emotional state.

After the press conference, Barry continued to employ social awareness in a private meeting with Detective Jacobs. By acknowledging the challenges faced by the investigative team and expressing unwavering support, he reinforced a sense of unity and purpose among his officers. This proficient navigation not only addressed external concerns but also bolstered internal resilience in the face of public scrutiny.

Barry's skillful use of self-awareness, self-management, and social awareness during the press conference exemplified effective leadership in a high-pressure situation. The delicate balance between transparency and reassurance demonstrated his commitment to both external communication and internal cohesion as the investigation progressed.

SECTION 4

Relationship Management

Sergeant's Slide

Sergeant Nick Warton had always been recognized for his sharp mind, disciplined approach, and unwavering dedication to his duties. When he finally received his promotion to sergeant, his fellow officers celebrated, confident that he would continue to lead with the same commitment that had defined his career. In the beginning, Nick lived up to those expectations.

The abandoned parking lot rumbled with energy as Nick took command. He held regular briefings with his officers during their downtime on the overnight shifts, listened attentively to their concerns, and maintained an open-door policy. His approachability and respect for his team created a positive atmosphere.

"Alright, everyone," Nick announced during one of the late meetings. "I want to hear your thoughts on how we can help detectives with the shooting from last weekend. Let's brainstorm together."

Officer Sarah Blake suggested, "Sarge, I think talking with the players in the area would be a start. I'm sure we can shake a few branches out there and see what comes out."

Nick nodded appreciatively. "Good idea, Sarah. Let's give it a shot. I'll coordinate with the other sergeants and see what we can do."

His proactive leadership style paid off, and the team saw improvements across the board.

However, as weeks turned into months, something shifted in Nick. The once neatly pressed uniform became wrinkled, his once meticulous desk now cluttered with paperwork, and his energized briefings turned into monotone recitations.

One night, Officer Jared Simmons approached him cautiously, having noticed the sergeant's absence during a chaotic scene earlier that evening. "Sarge, we've had a heck of a time getting in touch with you over the last few days. Is everything alright?"

Nick, with a hint of annoyance, responded, "Look, you and the team should be able to handle things on your own. I've got my own issues to deal with."

As the weeks passed, Nick's decline became more noticeable. His officers, accustomed to a leader who inspired them, found themselves in a precarious position. Morale waned, and productivity suffered.

After a particularly disheartening call for service where their sergeant was again nowhere to be found, Officer Teresa Jackson couldn't contain her frustration. "Sarge, what's going on? You're like a ghost. We have to go to Sergeant Lewis for everything now, and she's getting annoyed too."

Nick looked up, weariness evident in his eyes. "Look, things change. I've got a lot going on. You all need to figure it out yourselves."

Nick dialed Sergeant Nicole Lewis' number, frustration evident in his voice. "Nicole, it's Nick.", he sighed. "We've got a serious problem here. My people can't seem to get their act together."

Sergeant Lewis, audibly annoyed, responded, "Nick, we've discussed this before. You need to lead your team better. You need to actually be present and help them. You had them firing on all cylinders before. What's going on?"

"They're just not performing. It's like they've forgotten everything I've taught them," said Nick.

Sergeant Lewis sarcastically replied, "Maybe they need a reminder. Have you considered mentoring them more? It's part of the job, you know."

Nick responded with a breadth of defensiveness in his tone, "I've got a lot on my plate, Nicole. It shouldn't be my job to babysit them constantly."

"It's your job to lead them. If they're struggling, it's on you to guide and mentor. That's what being a sergeant is all about. You can't just leave them out to dry. This takes work," she replied with a firmness in her voice now.

Nick muttered, "Fine, fine. I'll see what I can do. But this shouldn't be solely my responsibility. What's the lieutenant doing? Isn't part of this on her?"

Sergeant Lewis impatiently and shortly responded, "It's not about placing blame, Nick. It's about ensuring your team succeeds. Step up and lead, or things will only get worse."

Nick sighed, realizing the truth in Sergeant Lewis' words. "Alright, I'll talk to them and see how I can help. But I still think they should know better."

The once-inspiring leader had transformed into a lackluster presence, leaving the officers feeling lost and unsupported. The teams' effectiveness plummeted, and their reputation in the department suffered.

One gloomy evening, as raindrops tapped rhythmically against his window, Nick sat slouched on his worn-out couch with a half-empty bottle of whiskey by his side. The flickering light of the muted television cast a dim glow on his disheveled appearance. His unkempt hair clung to his forehead, and the glow in his eyes seemed to have dimmed alongside his enthusiasm.

Across the city, the ambient sounds of traffic and distant sirens filled the air, but Nick was lost in the haze of his own discontent. The room felt stifling, a reflection of the stagnation that had taken root in his life. The whispers of missed opportunities and neglected responsibilities echoed through the quiet apartment.

On the other end of the phone, Nick's girlfriend, Rose Knight, sensed the change in his tone. The once lively conversations had evolved into a series of disconnected murmurs. She could feel the distance growing between them, masked by the facade of a shared movie night over the phone.

"Nick, is everything okay?" Rose's concern seeped through her words.

Nick sighed, the weight of his frustrations audible even through the phone. "I don't know, Rose. It just feels like I'm stuck in a rut. Work isn't what it used to be, and I can't find the motivation to get out of this funk."

Rose, sensing his vulnerability, tried to reassure him. "You know, everyone goes through tough times. Maybe it's just a phase. We can work through it together."

But Nick couldn't shake the persistent cloud that hung over him. The whiskey offered temporary solace, its warmth coursing through his veins, but it did little to dispel the shadows that lingered in his mind.

Nick, back at work the next night and recognizing the seriousness of the situation, decided to take immediate action to regain the trust of his officers. Eager to demonstrate his commitment, he called for another team meeting, hoping to reestablish the open communication and camaraderie they had once shared.

"Team," he began, "Let's bump up some of these numbers tonight. The lieutenant is getting on me, and I know we can do better."

The response, however, was noticeably subdued. Officer Simmons, who had previously been one of Nick's most vocal supporters, spoke up with a guarded tone, "Sarge, we've been running all week. I'm not sure that's what we need right now."

Nick, growing frustrated, asserted, "Look I know I've been absent, I'm here now, ready to lead. Let's put the past behind us and move forward."

Officer Blake sighed, "Sarge, listen to Simmons. We've been getting crushed and have a ton of paperwork to do."

The officers, lacking enthusiasm, slowly made their way back to their cars, uninspired by the presence of the sergeant.

Despite Nick's attempt to rally the team, the atmosphere remained tense and uneasy. Word of the team's decline reached Lieutenant Jessica Hayes, and she grew increasingly concerned about the impact on the department's overall performance. She decided to call Nick in for a meeting to address the issue.

A few days later, Nick received a stern message from Lieutenant Hayes, requesting his presence in an urgent meeting. As he walked down the hallway towards the lieutenant's office, he couldn't shake off the feeling of apprehension. The once proud and confident sergeant now found himself facing the consequences of his neglect.

When Nick entered the lieutenant's office, he was met with a stern expression. Lieutenant Hayes wasted no time getting to the point.

"Nick," the lieutenant began, her tone heavy with disappointment. "I've been receiving complaints from your officers about a decline in team performance and your lack of presence. Care to explain what's going on?"

Nick, feeling a mix of guilt and defensiveness, tried to explain himself. "Ma'am, I gave them everything I had when I first got them, and they were doing just fine. Now suddenly, they want me at every scene. This new generation is just different."

The lieutenant sighed, "Nick, your responsibility is to lead your team effectively. Not to slack off. You were once a shining example of leadership. What's happened?"

Nick struggled to find the right words. "I thought the team could handle things on their own for a while. I'm just tired of being on patrol."

Lieutenant Hayes leaned forward, her gaze intense. "Nick, you can't just abandon your responsibilities. Your team needs a leader, not someone who disappears when the going gets tough. Your officers are losing confidence, and it's affecting the entire squad."

Realizing the heft of the situation, Nick nodded solemnly. "I understand, ma'am. I will do whatever it takes to fix this and regain the trust of my team."

The lieutenant's expression softened slightly. "Good, because I believe you have the potential to be an excellent leader. But you need to address this issue immediately. I expect to see improvements, Nick, this isn't going to fix itself."

As Nick gathered his belongings at the office, Lieutenant

Hayes caught up with him just before he reached the exit. The lieutenant motioned for Nick to wait, concern etched on her face.

"Nick, mind holding on for a moment?" Lieutenant Hayes asked, his tone a mix of professional concern and genuine care.

Nick nodded, a hint of curiosity in his eyes as he lingered in the doorway.

The lieutenant gestured for him to step aside into a more private area of the hallway. Once there, she lowered her voice, "Nick, your well-being is just as important to me as your dedication."

Nick met the lieutenant's gaze, appreciating the sincerity in his superior's words.

Lieutenant Hayes continued, "I want to help you get back on track, both professionally and personally. I'm setting you up with Sergeant Brian Long. He's not just a seasoned officer. He's also our health and wellness coordinator. I think having someone to guide you in getting back into shape could be beneficial. What do you think?"

Nick, slightly taken aback by the unexpected turn of events, managed a grateful smile. "I appreciate that, ma'am. I could use a push in the right direction."

Lieutenant Hayes, with a playful grin, remarked, "Your 'yes' just saved you from becoming Sergeant Long's personal jiu-jitsu partner on our days off. He offered to give your neck a workout to make sure your head was screwed on tight—literally and figuratively."

Nick playfully shielded his neck and responded with an eye roll.

Lieutenant Hayes patted him on the back. "I've already spoken to Sergeant Long, and he's expecting you. Take this opportunity, Nick. Sometimes, a change in routine can make a world of difference."

As Nick left the lieutenant's office, he felt a mix of determination and regret. He knew he had let his team down, and now he had to find a way to rebuild what he had lost. The once-promising sergeant was faced with a daunting challenge – to rediscover the qualities that had earned him the respect of his officers and superiors alike.

Undeterred, Nick attempted to implement changes immediately, reinstating regular briefings and initiating new strategies. However, the officers, having experienced the recent decline in leadership, were hesitant to fully embrace the changes.

During a briefing, Officer Jackson, who had voiced her frustrations earlier, questioned the sincerity of the renewed efforts. "Sarge, is this just a temporary fix, or can we really count on you to be here for the long haul?"

Nick, realizing the depth of the skepticism, replied earnestly, "Look guys, I know I got lazy there for a while. But the lieutenant had a meeting with me and said I need to get things together. So here I am."

With his lackluster assurances, the officers remained wary, their trust shattered by the recent downturn in leadership. Rebuilding that trust would require more than just immediate changes—it would demand a sustained and unwavering commitment from Nick over an extended period. The once-unquestioned leader now faced the challenging task of proving himself anew to a team that had lost faith.

Navigating Bonds

This is the last riddle to unravel, the final piece of the EQ puzzle waiting for your masterful touch. Think of relationship management as the pivotal culmination of emotional intelligence. It represents your ultimate goal, encapsulating your ability to nurture and sustain positive connections with others. This skill involves adeptly navigating social dynamics, resolving conflicts, and fostering collaborative relationships—all of which are fundamental to being a great leader.

To attain proficiency in relationship management, you must progressively build upon the foundational facets of emotional intelligence we've been discussing, starting with self-awareness, followed by self-management, and complemented by social awareness.

I want to underscore that relationship management is a crucial necessity for effective police leadership. Whether you identify as introverted or not, recognize that your ability to build and maintain relationships is a keystone of great leadership. While the stereotypical image of a police leader often emphasizes authority and command, the reality is that successful leadership in this field hinges on your capacity to establish positive connections with your team members, the community, and various stakeholders.

DESPITE ANY PERSONAL INCLINATION TOWARD INTROVERSION, RECOGNIZE THAT YOUR EFFECTIVENESS AS A POLICE LEADER IS DEEPLY TIED TO YOUR ABILITY TO NAVIGATE AND MANAGE RELATIONSHIPS.

Consider the situation with Sergeant Nick Warton as an example. Sustaining relationships isn't always a straightforward task. It's a continuous, long-term effort that demands constant attention, much like tending to a fire. Allowing relationships to deteriorate is a definite way to impede the progress of an organization.

Internally, within the police force, relationship management plays a pivotal role in cultivating a cohesive and motivated team. Understand the individual strengths and challenges of your team members so you can tailor your leadership approach, fostering an environment of trust and respect. Effective communication and active listening become crucial tools for you to address concerns, provide guidance, and ensure the well-being of your officers.

Despite any personal inclination toward introversion, recognize that your effectiveness as a police leader is deeply tied to your ability to navigate and manage relationships. As an introverted leader you can harness your innate skills, such as thoughtful listening and decision-making, to build strong connections with your teams and communities. By prioritizing relationship management, you not only enhance the overall effectiveness of your law enforcement efforts but also contribute to the development of a positive and collaborative organizational culture.

In a field where public trust and teamwork are paramount, the ability to manage relationships becomes not just a leadership skill but a fundamental requirement for your success. Relationship management is the ultimate manifestation of the triad of emotional intelligence components. By developing self-awareness, mastering self-management, and refining social awareness, you lay the groundwork for establishing and sustaining robust, positive relationships.

Successful relationship management entails clear communication, empathy, conflict resolution skills, and the ability to collaborate effectively. As you hone these emotional intelligence skills, you become better equipped to navigate the complexities of human interaction, fostering healthier and more meaningful connections in both your personal and professional realms.

Primary Targets *for* Relationship Management

Fix It

Conflicting personalities and lingering issues within a police department are about as certain to occur as spilling coffee on yourself just before stepping into roll call. You've probably got a mental list of these eyebrow-raising moments and relationships as we speak.

I'm not advocating for you to become the department's unofficial relationship therapist, but let's make sure your own office dynamics are in check. Keep in mind, it's perfectly fine to encounter disagreements. Just ensure that you consider all the aspects we've covered so far when determining how you want to be perceived and the kind of relationships you aim to foster. Don't shy away from what must be addressed. Take the necessary steps to repair relationships that may have been strained for whatever reason over the years.

NAVIGATING THE INTRICATE DYNAMICS WITHIN A POLICE ORGANIZATION REQUIRES YOU TO STRIKE A DELICATE BALANCE OF LEADERSHIP, COLLABORATION, AND TRUST.

Navigating the intricate dynamics within a police organization requires you to strike a delicate balance of leadership, collaboration, and trust. Just as you instinctively know when you're on the right or wrong path in your personal life, this same intuition plays a pivotal role in your professional relationships within the force. As a leader, it's imperative for you to recognize the impact your actions have on the unity and cohesion of your teams. There are occasions when strained relationships may have surfaced within your domain, and as a leader, the responsibility rests on your shoulders to confront and attempt to resolve these situations. Don't wait for others to take the initiative. Seize the opportunity to foster a sense of camaraderie and mutual respect among your fellow officers and leaders.

Consider a scenario where conflicting approaches to policing strategies have led to tension among different units within the department. Instead of allowing these divisions to fester, take proactive steps to facilitate open communication channels. Organize roundtable discussions or training sessions where officers can share their perspectives, fostering a culture of collaboration rather than competition.

In another instance, if there are concerns about inconsistent leadership styles causing confusion and discontent, address these issues head-on. Implement leadership development programs that promote a unified approach and provide a forum for leaders to share best practices. By actively working to align leadership philosophies, you strengthen the foundation upon which the entire organization stands.

Lead by example in demonstrating the importance of trust and communication. Share your vision for the department, listen to the concerns and ideas of your fellow leaders, and create an environment where everyone feels valued. Building relationships within your organization is not just about addressing existing issues but also about creating a culture of continuous improvement and growth.

By acknowledging the existence of potentially strained relationships and taking proactive steps to address them, you not only enhance the working environment for your fellow officers but also contribute to the overall effectiveness of the department. Remember, a united front within the organization lays the groundwork for a police force that is resilient, adaptable, and truly effective.

First Name Basis

Enter our distinguished senior leader, a seasoned expert in leadership seminars and workshops. They've traversed the vast landscape of management theories and leadership doctrines, collecting wisdom like rare artifacts. However, when it comes to remembering the names of their team, they've adopted a more laissez-faire approach.

Sound familiar? I'll continue.

Picture them striding through the office corridors, armed with a wealth of leadership insights but navigating the sea of faces with a detached coolness. It's not that they can't remember names. It's just that in their world, names are like optional accessories—nice to have but hardly essential.

Every "Hey, you." is delivered with the confident nonchalance of a leader who's mastered the art of maintaining a certain mystique. In the dimension of this leader, it's not about forgetting, it's about embracing a leadership style that floats above the minutiae of names, leaving a trail of enigmatic encounters in their wake.

Being a police leader demands more than just overseeing operations. It requires a commitment to building genuine connections within your team and the community. One often overlooked yet profoundly impactful aspect is the effort it takes to know people's names. Let's be honest—it's not easy, especially in a dynamic and demanding environment. But let me tell you, the investment of time and energy to remember names pays off in the long run, making it an invaluable leadership skill.

Consider the leader who, despite the challenges of a bustling precinct, takes the time to learn and remember the names of every officer under their command. It's not a casual feat. It's a deliberate choice to foster a sense of respect and recognition within the team. This leader understands that in the hustle of daily police work, remembering names might seem like a small detail, but it's a powerful tool that forges connections and strengthens the fabric of your force.

Certainly, amid the myriad of responsibilities and pressures of police leadership, remembering names isn't the simplest undertaking. Nevertheless, the rewards are significant. Individuals will sense genuine appreciation, a form of currency that continues to yield returns.

INDIVIDUALS WILL SENSE GENUINE APPRECIATION, A FORM OF CURRENCY THAT CONTINUES TO YIELD RETURNS.

While it may take work, the benefit of knowing names is immeasurable. It's an investment in the roots of your organization and the bridge that connects you with your expanding team. Despite its challenges, persisting in this effort yields enduring dividends, rendering it a valuable decision for the sustained success of your leadership and the efficacy of your force in the long run.

Speak Up

Don't be an undercover compliment agent, the police supervisor who's mastered the art of silent praise. In their mind, they're a one-person standing ovation, but outwardly, they've got a Ph.D. in the ninja nod of approval. It's a comedy of unspoken commendations, where officers are left wondering if they just aced a mission or hallucinated a thumbs-up.

With that in mind, the importance of acknowledging and appreciating the efforts of your team cannot be overstated. Often, the simplest acts of recognition can have a profound impact on morale and team dynamics. Consider the power of expressing your appreciation when someone presents an idea effectively or excels in their duties.

If you find yourself impressed with the way someone, regardless of rank, has presented something or if you believe they've done an exemplary job, don't let that observation go unspoken. Taking a moment to convey your positive feedback is not just a nicety, it's a fundamental aspect of effective leadership.

People thrive on acknowledgment, and your words of encouragement can serve as a powerful motivator, fostering a culture of recognition and support within the force.

PEOPLE THRIVE ON ACKNOWLEDGMENT, AND YOUR WORDS OF ENCOURAGEMENT CAN SERVE AS A POWERFUL MOTIVATOR, FOSTERING A CULTURE OF RECOGNITION AND SUPPORT WITHIN THE FORCE.

Remember, silence can be a barrier to improvement. If you appreciate someone's contribution and keep it to yourself, they may never fully grasp the positive impact they've had. By expressing your commendation, you not only boost the individual's confidence but also reinforce the importance of quality work and dedication within the team.

It's easy to focus on what needs improvement or correction. However, taking the time to appreciate a job well done creates a positive feedback loop, encouraging individuals to continue striving for excellence. A culture of open acknowledgment and constructive praise contributes to a motivated and engaged team, ultimately enhancing the overall effectiveness of the police force.

Your words have the power to inspire, motivate, and uplift your team. If you witness commendable efforts, do not hesitate to express your appreciation. By doing so, you contribute not only to the personal development of your officers but also to the creation of a work environment where excellence is celebrated, and individuals feel valued.

Be Authentic

Hope aboard the imagination train one final time. A boisterous leader struts down the hallway, a smile plastered on their face like they're handing out free ice cream, but you can practically hear the gossip engine revving up when they turn around. It's like living in a real-life cop sitcom where every handshake comes with a side of side-eye. Their niceties are about as genuine as a rubber bullet, leaving everyone in the department with a collective eye-roll workout.

Avoid being that individual. It's as straightforward as that.

Being authentic is essential for successful relationship management, especially in leadership roles like law enforcement, and it directly involves you. Being authentic means presenting yourself sincerely, without any pretense or facade, and aligning your actions with your values and beliefs. In leadership, your authenticity becomes a powerful force that builds trust, credibility, and connection with both your officers and the broader community. Avoid attempting to counterfeit this. It's visible to everyone. Pretending to be authentic will only result in others distancing themselves from you even more.

AVOID ATTEMPTING TO COUNTERFEIT THIS. IT'S VISIBLE TO EVERYONE. PRETENDING TO BE AUTHENTIC WILL ONLY RESULT IN OTHERS DISTANCING THEMSELVES FROM YOU EVEN MORE.

It is crucial that you are transparent about your decision-making processes. Admit when you may not have all the answers and acknowledge the challenges your department faces. For instance, openly addressing issues such as officer misconduct, community concerns, or departmental shortcomings demonstrates your commitment to transparency, which is vital for building trust. Make sure your communication is authentic by sharing successes, attributing credit appropriately, and expressing gratitude. This creates a culture of openness and honesty within your organization. Your authenticity in relationship management also requires you to be true to yourself, even in the face of adversity. When you authentically express your values and beliefs, you set a clear example for your team. This consistency builds a foundation of trust because individuals can rely on you to act in accordance with your stated principles.

Also, your authenticity involves genuine empathy and a willingness to understand and connect with others on a personal level. Take the time to listen, learn, and respond with genuine care, demonstrating that you are approachable and genuinely invested in the well-being of those you lead. Your authenticity in relationship management is indispensable for effective leadership. By being true to yourself and your values, you create an environment where your officers and community members feel heard, respected, and confident in your commitment to fostering positive relationships. Ultimately, your authenticity is not just a leadership quality. It is a catalyst for building enduring connections and achieving success.

Dual Duties

Captain Luke Anderson cruised down the dimly lit highway, the city's hustle and bustle slowly fading into the background as he left the police department behind. The glow of streetlights painted a golden path ahead, and the soothing hum of his car engine mingled with the soft voices emanating from his car speakers. Luke was an avid fan of science-based podcasts, finding solace in the mysteries of the universe after a long day of dealing with the complexities of policing.

Tonight, he tuned in to his favorite podcast, *Cosmic Chronicles*, where the host delved into the wonders of the cosmos. As Luke listened to the mesmerizing tales of black holes and distant galaxies, he couldn't help but reflect on the chaotic day he had just experienced.

Earlier that day, the police department buzzed with activity as officers prepared for the day shift. Luke had the responsibility of delivering a brief speech to motivate his team during roll call. Navigating through a sea of uniforms, he took the stage, hoping to inspire confidence and unity among his officers. The pressure of leadership weighed on him, and he couldn't shake the nagging feeling that he might not have made the impact he intended.

Lost in thought, Luke's mind wandered to a particular moment during roll call. He had attempted to address each officer by their first name, a personal touch to foster camaraderie. However, one officer's name escaped him momentarily, causing a brief lapse in the otherwise smooth flow of his speech. Luke wondered

if anyone had noticed, especially the officer in question. Did his meeting with Corporal Frank Martin hit the mark? His mind raced. Only time would reveal the answer.

Was today just a one off for Lieutenant Megan Turner?

The podcast host's voice interrupted his introspection, announcing a fascinating discovery in the world of quantum physics. Luke's fascination with science momentarily distracted him from the events of the day, but as the podcast episode concluded, his mind returned to the uncertainties of his performance.

Luke then contemplated ongoing staffing shortages, a challenge that weighed heavily on his shoulders. He wondered if there was more he could do. If there were creative solutions to address the gaps in personnel. Perhaps there were untapped resources or alternative strategies to support his officers.

His thoughts then shifted to the well-being of his officers. The city's police force was more than just a collection of uniforms. It was a family facing challenges together. Luke hoped that despite the strains of the job, his officers knew the department was fully invested in their health and success.

The rhythmic drone of the tires on the pavement provided a steady backdrop to Luke's contemplation. As he continued down the highway, his mind danced between the mysteries of the cosmos and the intricacies of his responsibilities as captain.

Glancing at the city skyline in his rearview mirror, Luke couldn't help but recall the tumultuous city council meeting earlier in the day. The heated debates and impassioned pleas echoed in his mind.

His hand absently tapped on the steering wheel, and he dialed down the volume of the podcast, allowing the police radio to take center stage. The urgent voices from the radio hinted at the onset of a potential homicide investigation in a different part of the city. For a moment, Luke considered intervening, his fingers hovering over the radio controls. However, he resisted the urge. The fact that Lieutenant Jessica Hayes was on the air provided him with reassurance.

As the scene updates crackled through the speakers, Luke's mind drifted to the recent chief's press conference. The media had bombarded the chief with questions about recent incidents, demanding answers, and accountability. Luke recalled the careful balance the chief had to maintain, providing information without compromising ongoing investigations or the department's integrity.

Luke returned his attention to the road, the podcast now a distant murmur in the background. The city lights blurred into streaks as he pressed on, a metaphor for the blurred lines between his personal and professional life.

Pulling into his driveway, Luke turned off the engine, allowing silence to settle around him. He sat in the quiet darkness, replaying the events of the day in his mind. With a sigh, Luke stepped out of his car, the night air crisp and refreshing.

Luke stepped through the front door, his shoulders burdened by the invisible weight of the day's challenges. His wife, Grace, a woman in the midst of life's journey with brown hair gracefully embracing subtle gray strands, greeted him with a warm smile. Grace was well aware of the demands of his role, and her ability to read the unspoken emotions in his eyes made her an invaluable pillar of support.

Their two kids, Ryan and Emily, were seated at the kitchen

table, engrossed in their homework. Grace, a great multi-tasker and wizard with the kids, seamlessly balanced the responsibilities of managing both the household and the children's activities. Her brown eyes, filled with a blend of wisdom and kindness, reflected the countless times she had turned ordinary moments into cherished memories.

"Hey, Captain," Grace said playfully, using his work title to lighten the mood. "Tough day?" Her ability to inject humor into the routine moments of life showcased her innate skill at creating a warm and inviting atmosphere in their home, a sanctuary where Luke could find solace after facing the challenges of his demanding role.

Luke chuckled, shedding the seriousness of the day. "You have no idea. It's like a never-ending rollercoaster."

As he settled into the living room, Ryan and Emily couldn't contain their curiosity. "Dad, did you catch any bad guys today?" Ryan asked with wide eyes.

Luke ruffled Ryan's hair, his stern demeanor softening. "No bad guys today, bud. Just a lot of paperwork and meetings."

Emily, always insightful, chimed in, "Did you make any new friends, Dad?"

Luke laughed, appreciating Emily's innocence. "Well, not exactly. But I did my best to be the friendly captain everyone can count on."

Over dinner, Luke shared snippets of his day, carefully filtering the intensity of the job for the sake of his family. Grace listened attentively, her empathetic nature understanding the unspoken challenges. After dinner, Luke took a moment to sit with Ryan and Emily individually.

Ryan showed Luke his math homework, a sea of numbers that seemed to have multiplied since the captain's school days. Luke, with a patient smile, dove into the world of long division, offering encouragement and guidance. "You're doing great, bud. Just remember, every problem is like solving a little mystery."

With Ryan's homework conquered, Luke joined Emily on the couch, a picture book in hand. As he read, he animatedly brought the characters to life, captivating Emily's imagination. "Dad, you should be a storyteller," she beamed.

Later that night, after the kids were tucked into bed, Luke made a point to spend quality time with Grace. They sat on the porch, the evening breeze carrying away the remnants of the day. "How was your day?" Luke asked, genuinely interested.

Grace shared the highs and lows of her day as a schoolteacher, and Luke listened with the same attentiveness he gave his officers during roll call. He offered words of support, making sure Grace felt heard and valued. "I don't know how you deal with those gremlins," he laughed, a sincere admiration in his eyes.

In the calm of the evening, surrounded by the subtle sounds of night, Luke reflected on the power of connection within his own home. His leadership skills seamlessly transitioned to the domestic sphere, where dialogue, understanding, and shared moments reinforced the bonds that held them together. In the dual roles of police captain and family man, he continued to exemplify the principles of exceptional relationship management, creating a harmonious balance between the demands of work and the importance of connection at home.

Debrief

Relationship management, as exemplified by Captain Luke Anderson, extends far beyond the police department's walls, permeating every facet of life. Luke realized that the skills he developed as a police captain permeated beyond the scope of managing officers. They were invaluable in fostering meaningful connections within his own family. His ability to balance the demands of work and family life demonstrated the seamless integration of relationship management into his entire existence.

In the intimate setting of his home, Luke practiced open communication and empathy, two essential components of effective relationship management. He engaged with his children on a personal level, assisting with homework, sharing in their joys and curiosities, and becoming an active participant in their lives. By recognizing and addressing the unique needs of each family member, he reinforced the sense of trust and understanding crucial to any strong relationship.

Luke's relationship management skills extended further as he made deliberate efforts to connect with his wife, Grace. Taking the time to discuss her day, empathize with her challenges, and actively listen to her thoughts and feelings, he created a supportive environment that transcended the professional sector. This holistic approach to relationship management not only strengthened his familial bonds but also showcased the universal applicability of these skills.

Luke's actions underscored the idea that effective relationship management is not confined to the workplace. It is a dynamic and versatile skill set that, when practiced intentionally, can enhance personal connections, contributing to a well-rounded and fulfilling life. His ability to balance the challenges of police leadership with the joys of family life serves as a testament to the enduring impact of relationship management beyond professional spheres.

Moving Forward

Without a lofty conclusion or a compelling call to action, all I can offer is a humble aspiration. As you have navigated the pages of this book, my sincere hope is that it serves as a compass on your journey toward heightened emotional intelligence. Relationships, whether with family, friends, or colleagues, constitute the core of our existence. I hope you approach them with the gravity they merit, recognizing that these connections are the very underpinning of your life's narrative. This book is not a sermon but a guide, and I trust that you will use its insights to navigate the intricate terrain of emotions, enriching your bonds with others. After all, in the vast expanse of life, the quality of our relationships is the true measure of our wealth.

Reading Suggestions *and* Inspiration

Brackett, M. A. (2019). *Permission to Feel: Unlocking the Power of Emotions to Help Our Kids, Ourselves, and Our Society Thrive.* Celadon Books.

Bradberry, T. J., & Greaves, J. (2009). *Emotional Intelligence 2.0.* TalentSmart.

Brown, B. (2018). *Dare to Lead: Brave Work. Tough Conversations. Whole Hearts.* Random House.

Collins, J. (2001). *Good to Great: Why Some Companies Make the Leap and Others Don't.* Harper Business.

Goleman, D. (2009). *Emotional Intelligence: Why It Can Matter More Than IQ.* Bantam.

Goleman, D. (2002). *Primal Leadership: Realizing the Power of Emotional Intelligence.* Harvard Business Review Press.

Kouzes, J. M., & Posner, B. Z. (2017). *The Leadership Challenge: How to Make Extraordinary Things Happen in Organizations.* Jossey-Bass.

Maxwell, J. C. (2007). *The 21 Irrefutable Laws of Leadership: Follow Them and People Will Follow You.* Thomas Nelson.

Salovey, P., & Mayer, J. D. (1990). *Emotional Intelligence.* Imagination, Cognition, and Personality, 9(3), 185–211.

Willink, J., & Babin, L. (2015). *Extreme Ownership: How U.S. Navy SEALs Lead and Win.* St. Martin's Press.

About the Author

With a wealth of experience exceeding 15 years, Gene is a seasoned police officer who has demonstrated his skillset in various areas of policing, including investigative tasks, administrative duties, and supervision. His extensive experience has afforded him a comprehensive understanding of the complexities within the realm of law enforcement.

Gene holds a Doctorate in Criminal Justice, where his academic focus centers on resilience and stress management, shedding light on the psychological challenges faced by individuals in the field of law enforcement. This academic pursuit reflects his commitment to enhancing the well-being of fellow officers and contributing to the advancement of the criminal justice profession.

In addition to his doctoral achievements, Gene possesses a Master's degree in Education, showcasing his dedication to continuous learning and the development of skills beyond the traditional scope of law enforcement. His educational background also includes a Bachelor's degree in Public Safety Administration, providing a solid foundation for his multifaceted career.

Beyond his professional endeavors, Gene is a dedicated fitness enthusiast, where physical well-being holds a fundamental role in his life. He has not only incorporated fitness into his daily routine but has also illustrated his commitment to this lifestyle by successfully completing numerous triathlons, including the challenging Ironman Maryland. This accomplishment speaks volumes about his discipline, perseverance, and determination.

Most notably, Gene is a devoted family man. He is happily married to his wife, Abby, and is the proud father of two children, Laila and Luke. This commitment to family underscores the values that guide Gene both personally and professionally.

In his leisure time, Gene explores the art of Jiu-Jitsu, portraying a well-rounded approach to personal development and physical fitness. His diverse interests and achievements make Gene a unique and multifaceted individual, contributing not only to the law enforcement community but also to the broader spheres of education, fitness, and family life.

Made in the USA
Columbia, SC
07 February 2024